The Harmonized Gospel Story
of the
Four Scrolls

by Roxanne Tonkin

ISBN-978-1-7320169-1-0

LCCN- 2018903754

CONTENTS

NOTES

NOTES

NOTES

CHAPTER 1 — BIRTH & CHILDHOOD OF JESUS

The story of Jesus Christ began in the days of Herod, King of Judea — just as Rome was beginning to rule the world. There was an upright Jewish man whose name was Joseph (of the house of David; of the tribe of Judah). He was betrothed to a young Jewish virgin whose name was Mary. As Joseph toiled, building a home for them in Nazareth of Galilee, God (our heavenly Father) sent His angel (Gabriel) to speak to young Mary; to prepare her for what was to come. But when the angel appeared before her eyes, Mary was very much afraid. So, the angel said to her; "Fear not, Mary. You have found favor with God. You shall conceive in your womb and bring forth a Son and you shall call his name 'Jesus'. He shall be great, and shall be called the Son of the Highest. And the Lord God shall give him the throne of his forefather, King David. He shall reign over the house of Israel forever — and of his kingdom, there shall be no end." *(And all of these things would come to pass just as prophecy foretold that they would, in the book of Isaiah [9:7]).* **— (Luke 1:5-33)**

Confused; Mary asked the angel how this could possibly be (seeing that she and Joseph were not yet married). And the angel explained to her; "The Holy Ghost shall come upon you, Mary — and the power of the Highest shall overshadow you. Thereafter; that holy thing which you shall bear shall be called the 'Son of God'. And your cousin Elisabeth has also conceived a son, in her old age — and she is now six months pregnant (for, with God, all things are possible)." *(And Elisabeth's child, too, would grow up to serve a vital purpose in God's plan; for, Elisabeth's son would grow up to be none other than John the Baptist [Luke 1:5-25]).* And when Mary had carefully considered everything the angel had said, her heart was filled with awe and wonder. And Mary told the angel; "I am willing to serve the Lord; let it be exactly as you have said." — *(Luke 1:34-38)*

Immediately after the Holy Ghost had conceived in Mary's womb, she was stirred to go and visit her cousin, Elisabeth. And when her cousin heard the voice of Mary's greeting, the babe in Elisabeth's womb leaped and she was filled with the Holy Ghost. And Elisabeth immediately blessed her cousin Mary and the child in her womb. And Mary began to magnify the Lord, aloud, with praise. *(And Mary stayed with her cousin for three months; awaiting the birth of Elisabeth's child.)* — *(Luke 1:39-56)*

And in three-month's time, Elisabeth's child was born. Now, Elisabeth was married to Zacharias (who was a priest of Israel). And many months earlier, the angel Gabriel had also appeared to Zacharias — foretelling the conception and birth of this, their son; John. At that time, the angel had said to Zacharias; "When the child is born, you shall call his name John." And so, the moment Zacharias announced the name of his newborn son to be 'John', Zacharias was immediately filled with the Holy Ghost and began to prophecy — saying, of his newborn son; "You shall be called the prophet of the Highest. For, you shall go before the face of the Lord to prepare his ways; to give knowledge of salvation unto his people by the remission of their sins." And John would grow up in the Judean desert; he would grow stronger and stronger (in the spirit of Elias) until the day of his activation for Israel. *(This, too, would come to pass just as prophecy foretold that it would; in the books of Isaiah [40:3] and Malachi [3:1].)* — **(Luke 1:57-80 (& 1:5-25))**

Meanwhile: Immediately after John was born, Mary returned to her home in Nazareth (being three months pregnant with the Son of God). And when it was immediately obvious to the village (and to Joseph) that Mary was with child — unmarried and promised to Joseph — Joseph decided to break their engagement quietly (rather than having Mary stoned to death — which, was his right, in those days). But, as Joseph drifted off into sleep that night, the angel Gabriel appeared to him in a dream, saying; "Joseph, do not be afraid to take Mary as your wife; for, the child in her womb was conceived by the Holy Ghost. She shall bring forth a son, and you are to name him Jesus;

because he will save his people from their sins." *(The name 'Jesus' means 'Savior'.)* And when Joseph awoke from the dream, he faithfully did just as the angel had instructed him to do; without further delay, he made Mary his legal wife. — **(Matt 1:18-24)**

And in due course of time, Mary's child would be born. It would happen in the days when Caesar Augustus was Emperor of Rome; when (being stirred to issue a decree that all the world should be taxed by Rome) Caesar declared that every man must return to the city of his birth in order to pay his taxes. Now, Bethlehem *(the City of David)* happened to be the birthplace of Joseph. Therefore, it was to Bethlehem that Joseph must return (taking with him his wife, Mary, who was great with child by then). But because Bethlehem was so crowded with people (coming from all over the land, to pay their taxes), there were no empty rooms at any of the Inns in Bethlehem — and Mary and Joseph were forced to lodge in a barn when they arrived. Nevertheless; according to God's plan, the days of Mary's delivery were accomplished while they were there in Bethlehem — and on one particularly beautiful starlit night, the Son of God was born into the world.

Mary wrapped the babe in swaddling clothes *(which bound him hand and foot; as if in a cocoon)* and she lay him in a manger *(which was a feeding trough for the sheep)*. *(And Mary's actions were by no means random, on that night; God had orchestrated each of them, carefully. It was no coincidence that the baby Jesus' physical body was 'subdued' immediately upon entering the world — or, that his bound body was placed immediately into a feeding trough [from which, sheep are fed]. This was the method God had chosen for assuring mankind of His purpose for allowing His Son to be born into a human body.)* And Joseph called his name 'Jesus', just as the angel had commanded. *(And all these things had come to pass just as prophecy foretold they would, in the books of Micah [5:2] and Isaiah [7:14].)* — **(Matt 1:25 & Luke 2:1-7)**

And at that very hour — in a field just outside of Bethlehem — there were a group of shepherds keeping watch over their flocks, by night. And the angel Gabriel appeared before the shepherds — and he was surrounded by a brilliant light. The angel proclaimed, to the shepherds; "Do not be afraid; I bring you good tidings of great joy to all of mankind. For, today —

in the City of David — a Savior is born to you; which is Christ the Lord. And this shall be a sign for you; you will find your Savior bound in swaddling clothes and laying in a manger." With that, there appeared a multitude of angels surrounding the first angel — all of whom were praising God, saying; "Glory to God in the highest, and on earth peace and goodwill toward men." — *(Luke 2:8-14)*

And when the angels had finished proclaiming the Good News to the shepherds, they went away from them — back up into the heavens. And the shepherds raced down into Bethlehem and found their tiny Savior just as the angel had described — wrapped in swaddling clothes and lying in a manger. Unable to contain their joy, the shepherds began to run all around Bethlehem proclaiming the testimony of their visitation; how the angel had appeared to them in the field and proclaimed this child to be the Savior; Christ the Lord. — *(Luke 2:15-20)*

Meanwhile: in a land far to the east of Bethlehem, there were, on this very night, certain wise men who stood curiously observing the night sky — when they suddenly noticed the brilliant light shining over the Holy Land. Educated men *(and familiar with the Hebrew prophecy of Numbers 24:17 about the birth of Israel's promised 'Messiah')* they immediately recognized this luminous spectacle to be an authentic sign of his arrival. Therefore, they set out immediately for Jerusalem, to worship the newborn king of the Jews (whom, they fully expected had been born in the palace of King Herod, the king of Judea). However, this would be no short journey from their home. — *(Matt 2:1-2)*

And it came to pass, that when the baby Jesus was one month old (when the days of Mary's purification from childbirth were completed [Lev 12:1-7]) Mary & Joseph took the baby Jesus to the Temple in Jerusalem, to present him to the Lord (as was the custom of the people). Now, there was a priest in the Temple, named Simeon. And God had made a promise to Simeon — long ago — that he would see the Son of God born into the world, before he died. And on the day that Mary & Joseph entered into the Temple with the baby Jesus, Simeon took up the child into his arms and praised God, saying; "Lord, now let your servant depart in peace, according to your word — for I have seen your salvation for all people; a light to lighten the gentiles *(non-Jews)*, and the glory of your people Israel." Then, Simeon told Mary & Joseph; "This child is set for the fall and rising again of many, in Israel." And he told Mary; "A sword shall pierce through your own soul, also — that the thoughts of many hearts may be revealed." — *(Luke 2:21-38)*

Meanwhile; the wise men (from the East) had by now managed to follow the Messiah's brilliant, heavenly star all the way to the Holy Land *(although, no one knows for sure how long it took them to make the journey)*. But when they arrived in Jerusalem, they did not find the Holy child in King Herod's palace (as they had expected). *(Instead; they found a king who seemed oddly unaware of an event of such enormous significance to his people.)* King Herod ran quickly to consult with his priests and lawyers — then returned again to the wise men; inquiring of them when, exactly, they believed the child to have been born *(according to the first appearance of the brilliant star they had seen)*. And after the wise men answered the king's question, the king sent them to Bethlehem to find the child *(for, the prophecy of Micah 5:2 foretold Israel that their Messiah would be born in Bethlehem).* King Herod told the wise men to send word to him of the child's whereabouts when they found him, because he wanted to go and worship the new king, himself *(but this was not the truth).* — ***(Matt 2:3-8)***

And as the wise men left Jerusalem, they continued travelling toward the direction of the brilliant star they had followed all this way. They followed the star until the star was no longer in front of them — but, rather — directly above them. And they rejoiced with exceeding joy at the sign; having found the young child to be within the house the star had led them to. Entering into the abode, they saw the Christ-child with Mary and Joseph — and they knelt down before him to worship him. They gave him gifts from their treasures — gold and frankincense and myrrh. *(Now, the Bible doesn't actually tell us how many wise men visited the Christ-child on this day, but history has always presumed it to be 'three'; because there were three gifts offered that night.)* That evening — as the wise men lay sleeping — God warned them in a dream that they should not return to King Herod on their way home. So, when they rose up the next morning, they took a different route back to their own country. — *(Matt 2:9-12)*

Once the wise men had gone away, the angel appeared also to Joseph (in a dream); warning him; "Arise, and take the child and his mother, and flee into Egypt. Hide there until I come again and tell you that it's safe to return — because King Herod wants to kill the child." Therefore, Joseph arose and gathered his family quickly, and took them into Egypt, to hide. — *(Matt 2:13-15)*

And, as time began to pass *(weeks turning into months)*; King Herod eventually realized the wise men had discerned his dark intentions, somehow, and betrayed him. But this bloody king was not without alternative means to his end; he took swift (and brutal) action to assure the destruction of the little king — ordering that all baby boys of Bethlehem be killed, who were two-years-old and younger *(according to the time of the first appearance of the brilliant star the wise men had seen). (This, too, had come to pass just as it was foretold by prophecy, in the book of Jeremiah [31:15].)* — *(Matt 2:16-18)*

Now, as fate would have it; within three or four years' time, the bloody King Herod died. And, just as the angel Gabriel had promised, he reappeared to Joseph in a dream, saying; "Arise, take the child and his mother and go back into the land of Israel; for they who wanted to kill the child are dead." And Joseph made haste to obey the angel's command. But he was leery of Jerusalem — because King Herod's son now reigned in his father's place. Therefore; Joseph turned aside from Jerusalem and brought his family home to Nazareth (of Galilee). There, God would fill the child with wisdom, as he grew (for, the grace of God was ever upon him). — *(Matt 2:19-23 & Luke 2:39-40)*

Nevertheless; Joseph was obedient to the commandments of God, and gathered his extended family into a large caravan each year to bring them to the Temple in Jerusalem for the Feast of the Passover. And in the year that Jesus was twelve-years-old, we believe that God began to speak to his Son — for, as their caravan returned home from the feast that year, Jesus' parents discovered him missing from the group. Turning back again to Jerusalem, they found the twelve-year-old Jesus three days later — sitting in the Temple among the doctors; listening, and asking them questions. And everyone was astonished at Jesus' conversation. Now, his parents had searched for him for three long days before they finally found him — and his mother asked her Son; "Why have you frightened us like this?" But Jesus said to her; "Didn't you realize I must be about my Father's work?" Mary knew her son was not referring to the carpentry work of Joseph; she understood the meaning of his words — and she kept the saying in her heart. And Jesus returned home again with his parents, to Nazareth, because it was not yet his time. And he remained subject to his natural parents, as he grew. And God increased him, in spiritual wisdom and in physical stature, and he grew in favor with God and man. — *(Luke 2:40-52)*

Now, as it happened — some decades later — Rome had set in place a Roman Governor to rule over the Jews of Judea — and the Governor's name was Pontius Pilate. Beneath his authority there were three Jewish leaders over Israel (called, Tetrarchs) — which mediated over the various territories of the Jews. And the current Jewish Tetrarch ruling over the land of

Galilee, at this time, was Herod (the son of the long-dead King Herod). And it was in that day (in the fifteenth year of Tiberius Caesar) that the Word of the Lord came to John *(the cousin of Jesus)*; activating him to his purpose on this earth *(which was; to make the Son of God 'manifest' to mankind)*. And so, came *(a 30-year-old)* John the Baptist into all the country round about the Jordan River (in the desert of Judea) preaching the baptism of 'repentance' for the remission of sins. And God *(Himself)* had sent John *(the prophetic voice of Elias)* to cry out, saying; "Repent. The Kingdom of Heaven is near. Prepare the way of the Lord; make his paths straight. All flesh shall see the salvation of God." *(And this, too, had come to pass just as it was foretold by prophecy, in the book of Isaiah [40:1-5].)* — **(Matt 3:1-4 & Mark 1:1-3 & Luke 3:1-6)**

And the people from Jerusalem and all of Judea went out to listen to John preach. And upon hearing him, many became willing to repent of their rebellious and selfish mindset. Willing to part from sin, they followed John's instruction; they confessed their sinful nature before God, and were water-baptized in the Jordan River (exactly as the Father had instructed, through John). *(To submit their body to water-baptism [in the name of the Father; according to the process He designed], they were sacramentally preparing their condemned 'fleshen'-soul for the pardon that would become available at the moment of Jesus' death. This sacrament is the one-and-only mechanism the Father designed for this particular function.)* For, John himself said; "I baptize you with water unto repentance for the remission of sins *(that are past [Rom 3:25])*. But another man (mightier than me) will come after me — baptizing you with fire & Holy Spirit *(making you a new creature)* — *(see the three-part baptism in Acts 19:1—6)*." And as John water-baptized the Jews of Israel, he made sure they understood that God expects them to go forward bringing forth the fruits of God's love among their fellow man (from that time, forward) or, they would be cut off from God again. And many other things did John preach to the people — to prepare their souls to receive Christ *(when he was finally manifested)*. — **(Matt 3:5-12 & Mark 1:4-8 & Luke 3:7-18) & (Rom 3:23-29 & 2 Corinth 5:17 & John 1:12)**

And this is how we know that the testimony of John was true: Because the angel of the Lord told his Father (before John was born); "Fear not, Zacharias; thy wife Elisabeth shall bear thee a son, and thou shalt call his name John. And John shall be filled with the Holy Ghost, even from his mother's womb. And many of the children of Israel shall John turn to the Lord their God. And John shall go before the Lord in the spirit and power of Elias *(which is to say, 'prophecy')* to turn the disobedient mind to the wisdom of the just; to make ready a people prepared for the Lord." — *(Luke 1:13-17 & John 1:6-9)*

Now, as all the Jewish people were being water-baptized by John in the Jordan River, it came to pass that Jesus also came unto John — and *(making himself know to him)* asked John to water-baptize him. But John refused to water-baptize Jesus. John understood his own need to be baptized by the Son of God — but in his ignorance, he didn't realize that *(just like every other fleshen-soul)* the condemned physical flesh that Jesus wore needed to be *(physically)* water-baptized. *(John didn't understand that just as fire-baptism performs a necessary function of grace [upon the*

spiritual 'heart'] — so, too; water-baptism performs a
necessary function of grace [upon the physical
'Soul']. And both functions are critical to God's
salvation plan [see Acts 19:1—6]. The miracle-works of
God would manifest through Jesus only after his flesh
was water-baptized. In other words; the 'spiritual'
Son of God was indeed sinless—[i.e.; the 'heart' of
Jesus] — but the flesh that he wore was condemned
[because, 'what is born of the spirit is spirit, and
what is born of flesh is flesh'—(John 3:6)]. This was,
after all, the whole purpose for the Son of God to be
born into flesh [becoming our fleshen brother]; so
that he could pay the exact fleshen debt we owed.)
After Jesus explained to John that he must be water-
baptized in order to fulfill 'all' righteousness *(to*
make 'all' things right); only then, did John agree to
water-baptize Jesus. And immediately when Jesus was
raised up out of the water, Jesus began to pray. And
the heaven was opened to him, and the Holy Ghost
descended upon him as a dove and lighted upon him, and
remained upon him *(anointing him with the full power*
from on high). And the voice of God spoke aloud, for
all to hear; claiming Jesus as His own beloved Son

(Christ, the Son), in whom He was well pleased. *(And John was the Holy-Ghost-filled-witness who bear record that Jesus was Christ, the Son of God. And, both Jesus & John were 30-years-old when they were activated for the Kingdom of Heaven.)* — **(Matt 3:13-17 & Mark 1:9-11 & Luke 3:21-23 & John 1:14-15)**

Immediately after his water-baptism, Jesus was led by the Spirit into the wilderness of ungodly man. There, Jesus fed his physical body nothing for forty days *(while God, the Father, fed his spirit instead)*. And after forty days — at the height of his physical & mental vulnerability — Satan approached him to tempt him, saying; "If thou be the Son of God, command that these stones be made bread *(he was trying interrupt God's 'spiritual' feeding schedule)*." But Jesus told Satan that God promised man spiritual food (through His Word) in addition to physical food — quoting the scripture. And the enemy could not overcome this Word. Next; Satan tried to use the written promises of God to puff up Jesus' pride — to cause him to test his God. *(This was the same temptation the evil one had lain before the nation of Israel; to destroy them.)* But Jesus told Satan that the Word of God also says,

'Do not tempt the Lord your God' *(Jesus was weighing precept upon precept).* And the enemy could not overcome this Word. Lastly; Satan promised to give Jesus the whole world, right now — if Jesus would simply bow down and worship him *(instead of God).* *(This is the same temptation the Devil has laid before all of mankind; hoping to destroy us.)* But Jesus answered him; "Get behind me, Satan: for the scripture says, 'you shall worship the Lord your God, and him only shall you serve'." And the enemy could not overcome this Word. And when Jesus had overcome the Devil these three times (using the Word of God against him), the Devil fled from Jesus — and angels came and ministered to Jesus. — *(Matt 4:1-11 & Mark 1:12-13 & Luke 4:1-13)*

Having successfully resisted Satan, Jesus returned again to John (in Judea) — who, stood answering questions of all those which had been sent to learn who 'John the Baptist' was. And as John stood earnestly contending that he was not the 'Christ' — but rather; the voice of one crying in the wilderness to prepare the way of the Lord — Jesus appeared before him in the crowd. The moment John saw Jesus in the crowd, he immediately identified Jesus as the true 'Lamb of God' in the midst of Israel. He validated his declaration by explaining that God himself had told him how to identify the Messiah: John said; "I saw the (Holy) Spirit descending from heaven like a dove, and it abode upon him. And I knew him not: but He that sent me to baptize with water had said to me, 'upon whom thou shalt see the (Holy) Spirit descending and remaining on him, he is the one which baptizes with the Holy Ghost'. And I saw, and bear record that this is the Son of God." (This event took place in Bethabara, beyond Jordan River; where John had been baptizing.) The following day, John pointed Jesus out again as he walked among the crowd. This time, a fisherman named Andrew heard the announcement and ran to find his brother Simon (Peter). And the two men began to follow after Jesus *(because the voice of the Holy Spirit, within John, had said this was the 'Messiah', and their ears were willing to hear it).* And this was the first day of Jesus' three-year salvation ministry. — *(John 1:19-42)*

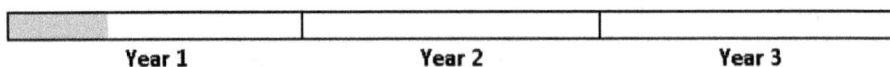

Year 1	**Year 2**	**Year 3**

The following day, Jesus departed from Judea, going forth into Galilee. As he traveled north, he came upon a man named Philip. He said to Philip; "Follow me." (And Philip ran immediately to find his friend Nathanael; joyfully inviting him to come and meet the Messiah, too.) Now, Jesus 'knew' Nathanael before they were even introduced *(Jesus, having foreknowledge)* — and when this became known to Nathanael it convinced him that Jesus was, in fact, the Messiah. And Jesus told Nathanael that hereafter, he would see heaven open and the angels of God ascending and descending upon the Son of man. — *(John 1:43-51)*

On the third day of Jesus' salvation ministry, there was a marriage in Cana of Galilee, and Mary (the mother of Jesus) was there. She invited Jesus and his disciples into the marriage feast. When they asked Mary for some wine to drink, Mary told them all the wine was gone, already. But then she turned to Jesus and asked him to provide more wine for the guests. At first, Jesus seemed reluctant to use the power of his anointing in this way — but ultimately he complied with her request and turned the contents of six

waterpots into wine, that day. And the governor of the
feast attested that it was exceptional wine. This
manifestation of Jesus' Glory was the beginning of his
miracles; and his disciples believed on him. *(It is
noteworthy that these verses reveal Jesus had never
performed a 'miracle' until after his condemned
physical flesh was water-baptized.)* From there, Jesus
travelled on toward Capernaum — he and his mother Mary
and his brothers (James, Joses, Simon & Judas [Matt
13:55]) and his disciples (Andrew, Simon [Peter],
Philip & Nathaniel) — and they would dwell in this
area for a time *(they made Capernaum their 'home-base'
during Jesus' ministry on Earth).* — *(John 2:1-12)*

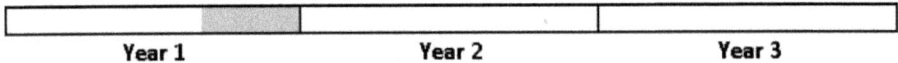

Year 1	Year 2	Year 3

And when the Jewish Feast of the Passover was at
hand, Jesus went up to Jerusalem. *(This event marked
the end of his first year of ministry.)* There, he
found the Temple of the Lord filled with merchants,
and he began to wreck their tables and chase them out
of the Temple. He rebuked them for making his Father's
house of worship into a den of thieves. The Jews,
therefore, demanded to know by what authority Jesus

presumed to 'rule' the Temple. Jesus stated, simply; "Destroy this Temple and I will raise it up again in three days." *(Jesus was alluding to the strength of his authority — but it was not yet time for them to understand that saying.)* But many believed on his name in that day; having witnessed the deeds which he did, there in Jerusalem. — *(John 2:13-25)*

And there was a Pharisee of Israel named Nicodemus who came to Jesus by night, asking sincere questions of him. And Jesus told him; "Except a man be born again, he cannot see the Kingdom of God; except he be born of water and of the Spirit, he cannot enter into heaven — because, what is born of the flesh is flesh, and what is born of the spirit is spirit. But if you can't understand the earthly things I tell your people, how can you believe in heavenly things? Moses lifted up the serpent in the wilderness. So, also, must the Son of man be lifted up; that whosoever will believe in him shall have eternal life. For God loved the world so much, that he gave up his only begotten Son — so that the world, through his willing sacrifice, might be saved. Whoever does not believe this, is condemned already. And this is the condemnation; that light is come into the world, but men loved darkness rather than light because their deeds were evil and they did not want to be reproved. But everyone who performs truth is willing to come to the light so that their deeds may be made manifest; that they are wrought in God." – *(John 3:1-21)*

Afterward, Jesus and his disciples left Jerusalem and entered back into the land of Judea. There, Jesus communed with his disciples and baptized. And John the Baptist also baptized nearby *(for he was not yet cast into prison)*. And soon there arose a question among John's disciples; why did Jesus also baptize people? And John spoke, saying to them; "A man can receive nothing except it be given by God. I told you before that I am not the Christ; he that has the bride is the bridegroom. I am but the friend of the bridegroom. I rejoice to listen to his voice; this fulfills my joy. Jesus must increase, while I must decrease. I speak of earthly things, while Jesus speaks of heavenly things. He who *(willingly)* receives Jesus' testimony has already set his seal that God is true. He whom God has sent speaks the Words of God — and God does not give him the spirit sparingly. The Father loves his Son,

and has given all things into his hand. He who
believes in the Son has eternal life, but the wrath of
God will abide upon he that does not believe the
testimony of Jesus." *(John was explaining to his own
disciples that they must continue beyond the limited
water-baptism (of the 'physical' soul) that John
himself provides; they must then become fire-baptized
disciples [of Jesus' 'spiritual' heart] [see Acts
19:1—6]; wherein, John's loss becomes Jesus' gain
[just as the process was designed to function].)* –
(John 3:22-36)

And in due course of time; when the Holy Spirit
knew the Pharisees of Israel had heard about Jesus'
disciples baptizing more disciples than John did (and
Herod had, by now, cast John into prison [Luke 3:19]),
therefore; the Holy Spirit stirred Jesus to leave
Judea *(southern Holy Land)* for Galilee *(northern Holy
Land)* for the second time in his salvation ministry;
to begin preaching the Gospel of the kingdom. Now, as
they were passing through the land of Samaria *(heading
north)*, Jesus took rest upon the side of Jacob's well.
When he did, a Samaritan woman came to draw water from
the well. So, Jesus began to speak to her. When he

did, the woman questioned Jesus' purpose in speaking to her *('Samaritans' were half-breed Jews who were considered 'unclean' for true Jews to associate with. Therefore, she was not accustomed to a Jew speaking with her)*. Jesus said to her; "Whoever drinks the water from this well, will thirst again. But whoever drinks of the water that I have, to give, he will never thirst again; the water I give will become, inside of him, a well of water springing up into everlasting life." And the woman immediately asked Jesus to give her this 'living water'. Instead, Jesus began to recite to the woman her history of fornication and her current sinful living arrangement. Perceiving that he was a 'prophet', she began to complain to him that her people *(the Samaritans; half-breed Jews)* are forbidden to go to the Temple in Jerusalem to worship God. But Jesus comforted her; he told this Samaritan woman the day was fast approaching when God's true worshippers would worship Him in their hearts — in spirit and in truth — rather than in a building. He explained that the Father seeks such as those, to worship Him, because He is 'spirit'. Eventually, Jesus told the woman plainly that he is

the Messiah who was prophesied to come. — *(Matt 4:12 &
Mark 1:14-15 & Luke 4:14 & John 4:1-27)*

With that, the Samaritan woman stood up and ran
into the city to tell the men; "Come and see a man who
told me all things ever I did — is not this the
Christ?" And the men came forth, to speak with Jesus.
And many Samaritans came to believe on Jesus, because
the woman proclaimed him to be the Christ, and they
were willing to hear it. And they asked Jesus to
commune with them a while, in Samaria. Jesus stayed
with them for a couple of days, and many more
Samaritans came to believe on him because of his own
Words to them; believing that he is Christ, the Savior
of the world. And at some point Jesus' disciples
discerned that he had not been eating — so, they began
to question him. But he told his disciples; "I have
meat to eat that you know not of; my meat is to do the
will of him that sent me, and to finish his work. Lift
up your eyes, and look on the fields; for they are
ready to harvest. And he that reaps receives wages,
and gathers fruit unto life eternal; that both, he
that sows the seeds, and he that reaps the fruit, may
rejoice together; One sows, and another reaps. I sent

you to reap where you bestowed no labor; other men labored — and you are entered into their labors." Then Jesus departed Samaria, continuing out into Galilee *(heading further north)*. — *(John 4:28-43)*

And when Jesus entered into Galilee the second time, the Galileans welcomed him home. This time, many of the inhabitants had personally witnessed deeds which Jesus had performed, in Jerusalem; during the Feast of the Passover. Once again, Jesus came into Cana *(where he had performed his first miracle; turning the water into wine)*. Now, there was a nobleman from Capernaum whose son was sick (nearly to the point of death) who, upon hearing that Jesus was nearby, sent and asked Jesus to come to Capernaum to heal his son. Jesus replied; "Go your way; the boy is healed." And the man believed Jesus' words, and went home. And when he arrived, he found that the boy had, indeed, been healed; in the very hour the words were spoken from Jesus' lips. And the nobleman believed. And his whole house believed. *(This was the second miracle Jesus performed after being water-baptized.)* — *(John 4:43-54)*

And upon entering Nazareth *(where Jesus grew up)* he went into the Synagogue on the weekly Sabbath day, and stood up to read. He opened the book of Isaiah to where it is written; "The Spirit of the Lord is upon me, because he hath anointed me to preach the Gospel to the poor; he hath sent me to heal the broken hearted, to preach deliverance to the captives and recovering of sight to the blind, to set at liberty them that are bruised (Gen 3:15) and to preach the acceptable year of the Lord." Then Jesus closed the book, and said to them; "This day, is this scripture fulfilled in your ears." And he began to tell his neighbors that not everyone would be healed and saved. He intended to go on (to explain that salvation would require great faith, and not everyone had it), but the Nazarenes rose up suddenly and cut him off; thrusting him out of Nazareth. They were unable to see past his flesh and bones — no matter the miracles he performed. In their minds, Jesus was the Son of a Nazarene carpenter from their village, and he was no 'great one' to come tell them that some of them wouldn't be counted 'worthy', by God. Therefore, Jesus and his disciples departed Nazareth; heading on to Capernaum, to preach the Kingdom of God. — *(Matt 4:13-17 & Luke 4:15-30)*

And as Jesus walked and preached along the Sea of Galilee on the coast of Gennesaret, he found himself pressed by the multitudes of people. And seeing Simon (Peter) and Andrew cleaning their nets in the sea *(for they were fishermen from Galilee — and they fished, when they were home)*, he asked them to stop their own work and take him out (in their fishing boat) — just off shore a little ways — so he could safely preach to the people, from the sea. Willing to serve him, Simon (Peter) and Andrew immediately did what Jesus asked of them. And when Jesus was finished preaching to the crowds that day, he turned to his faithful servants and bid them cast their nets into the sea, and their nets were immediately filled with fish (to the point of breaking). So, they called out to their partners for help, and James and John came to the aid of their friends. And Simon (Peter) fell down at Jesus' knees, saying; "Depart from me; for I am a sinful man, O Lord (for he was astonished at the volume of fish that were provided)." And Jesus said to them; "Follow me, and I will make you fishers of men." And they left everything and followed Jesus (James and John leaving their Father Zebedee on the boat, with the hired servants). *(It's interesting to note, here, that when Simon and Andrew originally began 'following' Jesus [John 1:40-42], they hadn't technically been 'called', yet. The account given in the passage just above is the point where Jesus actually 'called' them into his ministry.)* **— (Matt 4:18-22 & Mark 1:14-20 & Luke 5:1-11)**

And when they finally entered into the city of Capernaum (on the weekly Sabbath day), Jesus went immediately into the Synagogue and began to preach the Gospel of Truth. They who listened were astonished at his doctrine and delivery; because he taught as someone having authority (not as a mere scribe). Then suddenly, a man rose up in the audience (possessed by an unclean spirit). Recognizing Jesus to be the Son of God, the unclean spirit cried out to Jesus; "Leave us alone. Have you come to destroy us? I know who you are, Holy one of God." And Jesus rebuked the spirit, saying; "Hold your peace and come out of him." So, the unclean spirit threw the man's body to the floor, and came out of him. And those who witnessed the event were amazed at Jesus' authority; that even unclean spirits obeyed his voice. — *(Mark 1:21-28 & Luke 4:31-37)*

When they left the Synagogue that first day, they entered into the home of Simon (Peter) and Andrew, along with James and John. And Simon (Peter's) mother-in-law was very ill. But when they told Jesus of her condition, Jesus came to her and took her by the hand — lifting her up — and immediately, the fever left her and she began to serve them. When the evening came, they began to bring to Jesus all the diseased and possessed people of the land; all the city gathered at their door. And as Jesus healed the sick and cast out devils, he forbad the devils to speak (because they knew him). The next morning, Jesus departed to a desert place to pray — and when the people came and found him there, he said to them; "I must preach the Kingdom of God to other cities also: for, that is what I have come to do." And so he did preach in the Synagogues throughout all of Galilee. — *(Matt 8:14-17 & Mark 1:29-39 & Luke 4:37-44)*

And in a certain city, a leper came and knelt down before Jesus and said; "If you are willing, you can heal me." And Jesus was willing — so he healed him. And he charged the man not to spread the story abroad; but, to go and show himself to the priest. But the man so publicized the matter that Jesus had to avoid the city because of the multitudes that thronged him, there. — *(Matt 8:1-4 & Mark 1:40-45 & Luke 5:12-16)*

And when they returned again to their home-base in Capernaum, Jesus continued to preach to the multitudes there. And it came to pass, on a certain day, that there were present Pharisees and Lawyers of Israel from out of every town of Galilee and Judea and Jerusalem. And some men brought a fellow stricken with Palsy, to be healed — but they could not reach Jesus for the press of the multitudes around him. So, they went upon the housetop and lowered the man down through the roof, into the midst of Jesus. When Jesus saw their faith, he said to the man; "Your sins be forgiven you." And with that, the Lawyers and Pharisees of Israel began to accuse Jesus of blasphemy (because, only God can forgive sins). But Jesus said to them; "So that you may know that the Son of man has power on the earth to forgive sins, I say to this man,

'Arise, and take your bed home'." And the man immediately came to his feet and took his bed home. And many glorified God, that day. — *(Matt 9:1-8 & Mark 2:1-12 & Luke 5:17-26)*

As Jesus passed forth from that place, he saw a tax collector named Matthew sitting at his booth — and he bid him; "Follow me". And Matthew followed Jesus. And as he continued walking along the shore of the Sea of Galilee he saw another tax collector, named Levi *(a son of Alphaeus...which, Matthew was not [Mark 2:14, Matt 10:3, Luke 6:15, Mark 3:18 & Acts 1:13])* who was sitting at his booth. And he bid him; "Follow me." And Levi rose up and left everything to follow Jesus. And he prepared a great feast for Jesus (and a great multitude of other tax collectors and family and disciples) in his own home. And when the Lawyers and Pharisees of Israel murmured against Jesus' disciples (because they ate with tax collectors and sinners), Jesus said to them; "Those who are healthy do not need a physician — but rather; those who are sick. I did not come to call the righteous; I came, to call sinners to repentance." *(Jesus was saying that he didn't come into the world to socialize with righteous people; he came, to teach poor lost sinners that repentance and salvation are not beyond their reach; that he prefers to exchange mercy for sincere repentance rather than to inflict retribution for broken rules.)* Jesus told these Lawyers and Pharisees of Israel that they should go and try to learn what that means — and stop condemning the guiltless. *(Jesus had come into the earth to set the captives free — not to condemn them.)* **— (Matt 9:9-13 & Mark 2:13-17 & Luke 5:27-32)**

Then came the disciples of John the Baptist to ask Jesus why Jesus' disciples do not fast *(from food)*, like John's disciples do.*(John's disciples were water-baptized men who had repented under Old Testament Law — but, they were not yet 'believers' of Jesus' New-Testament Covenant.)* Jesus explained to John's disciples that the bridegroom *(Christ the Son)* is already present with his own disciples — so, there was no need for them to fast (to draw nearer to him). But, he said; "The days will come, when the bridegroom *(Christ the Son)* will be gone from earth again — and in those days, my disciples will fast for me, again." **— (Matt 9:14-17 & Mark 2:18-22 & Luke 5:33-39)**

```
┌─────────────────┬─────────────────┬─────────────────┐
│                 │                 │                 │
└─────────────────┴─────────────────┴─────────────────┘
     Year 1            Year 2            Year 3
```

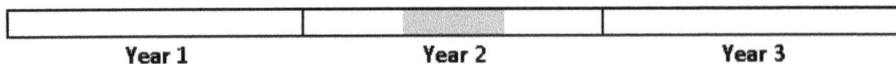

After this, there was a Feast *(of Tabernacles? in September?)* in Jerusalem — and Jesus went up to Jerusalem at that time. And there was a pool in that city called, 'Bethesda' — wherein (from time to time) an angel would stir the waters, and whosoever would first touch the water, thereafter, would be healed of whatever disease he might have. Many impotent folk lay around the pool daily, hoping to be healed. And there was a crippled man among the crowd one day, who was unable to bring himself to the water's edge. Therefore, Jesus (already knowing the man's history) asked the man his purpose there. After the crippled man explained aloud that he was unable, of himself, to get to the water to be healed, Jesus said to him; "Rise; pick up your bed and walk." And so the man did. *(And Jesus had healed the man who confessed aloud that he could do nothing to heal himself.)* But, because this healing took place on the Sabbath day, the Jews began to persecute Jesus. So, Jesus told them; "My Father *(the Spirit of Goodness/Truth)* works on the Sabbath — and so do I." Then the Jews wanted to kill

him, because he said God was his Father (making
himself equal with God). — *(John 5:1-18)*

Therefore, Jesus began to testify of himself: He
said; "The Son *(Goodness & Truth, the Son)* can perform
nothing of his own power — only what the Father
(Goodness & Truth, the Father) is able to perform and
wants the Son to perform as well; the Son does those
things. And because the Father loves the Son, he shows
him all these things. And greater things still, will
He show him — so that you can marvel. For as the
Father gives life back to the dead, even so does the
Son; to whomever he chooses. For, the Father has
committed all judgment to the Son, so that all men
should honor the Son *(Goodness & Truth, the Son)* as
well as the Father *(Goodness & Truth, the Father)*. And
whoever does not honor the Son doesn't honor the
Father who sent him. Here is truth: anyone who hears
my Words and believes on the Father, who sent me, will
pass from death back into life, having no
condemnation." — *(John 5:19-24)*

*(All these things, Jesus preached, so that the
lost children of God could begin to understand what
their Father had set in motion upon the earth, to save*

them.) And Jesus continued to preach, saying; "Here is truth: the hour has arrived, wherein, the dead *(in their sins)* shall hear the voice *(truth)* of God — and they that *(are willing to)* hear shall find life. For, just as the Father has life in himself *(the eternal Holy Spirit of Truth)*, so has he given the Son life in himself — and authority; because he is the Son *(the image of the Father)*. The hour is coming when all of the dead shall hear God's voice and come forth. Those who have done good will be resurrected into life, and those who have done evil will be resurrected into damnation." *(Some Christians believe there will only be a resurrection of the 'saved' souls — while convinced that there will not be a resurrection of the 'damned' souls. The verses above clearly dispel that erroneous conclusion. Them damned will be resurrected from the grave and then cast into the Lake of Fire to burn for eternity with the dark angels.)* Jesus went on to say; "I can perform nothing of myself — but as I hear from God, I judge. And my judgment is just; because I do not represent my own *(free)* will — but rather; the *(Good)* will of my Father who sent me. I do not bear witness of myself, but the Holy Spirit bares witness of me. You inquired of John the Baptist, and he bear witness to the truth. I'm telling you these things so that you might be saved. John the Baptist was a burning and shining light for you — and you were willing *(during that season of enlightenment)* to rejoice in his light. But I have a greater witness than that of John the Baptist; for the works that my Father gave me to finish — the works that you witness me performing *(proclaiming God's Word, healing, etc...)* — they bear witness of me, that the Father has sent me." — *(John 5:25-36)*

Then Jesus began to rebuke the non-believers among them, saying; "The Father, Himself — who sent me — has born witness of me. You have not seen or heard from Him. Nor, do you have His Word living and growing inside you; for, you do not believe me, whom He has sent. Search the scriptures; when they *(the Old Testament Words)* offer you hope of a Savior to come, they testify of me. Yet, you will not come to me, that you might be saved. I receive no honor from men, but I know that your hearts do not have the love of God, within. I am come in His name *(as a 'Savior')* and you will not have me. But, if someone comes to you in his own name; him, you will trust and accept. How can you believe; you, who are content to receive honor from one another but see no need to seek the honor that comes from God? Do not fear that I will accuse you to my Father — for, it is Moses *(Old Testament Law)* who accuses you to Him; Moses, in whom the fate of your people is trusted. But if you had truly believed *(accepted)* Moses, you would believe me — because he wrote of me. And if you cannot truly trust his words *(the Old Testament scriptures)*, how can you possibly trust my words *(the New Testament Gospel)*?" — *(John 5:37-47)*

And it came to pass, on a weekly Sabbath day, that as Jesus and his disciples walked through the corn fields they began to pick ears of corn *(to eat)*. And the Pharisees of Israel began to accuse them of breaking the law *(doing work, on the Sabbath)*. But Jesus told them; "Have you not read that when King David and his men needed food, they went into the house of God and ate the showbread (which, was lawful only for the priests to eat)? The Sabbath was made for man — not the man, for the Sabbath. Therefore, the Son of man rules over the Sabbath." And he told them again that he values mercy in place of rules and retribution — and that if they understood this, they would not have condemned the guiltless. *— (Matt 12:1-8 & Mark 2:23-28 & Luke 6:1-5)*

That said; Jesus and his disciples entered into the Synagogue. And there was a man inside with a withered hand. And the Pharisees of Israel watched Jesus to see if he would also heal the man's hand (on the Sabbath). And, so (knowing their evil thoughts) Jesus asked a question aloud, saying; "Is it lawful on the Sabbath days to do good, or evil; to save life, or to destroy it?" Receiving no answer from the crowd, he healed the man's hand. Jesus wanted to make the point that it's never wrong to do 'good' *(neglect or injustice were never the goal or intention of God's Law.)* But the Pharisees were unable to see the truth of his wisdom. Instead, they were filled with madness and took council against him; how they might kill him. *— (Matt 12:9-14 & Mark 3:1-6 & Luke 6:6-11)*

CHAPTER 2 — JESUS BEGINS TEACHING IN NORTHERN ISRAEL

Then Jesus and his disciples left Jerusalem; returning to the Sea of Galilee *(heading north, again)*. And a great multitude followed with him, from Judea and Jerusalem and many other lands. These, he healed and cleansed of unclean spirits (which, fell down before him; obeying his authority). And after being thronged by the pressing crowds all day, Jesus retreated to a mountain place to pray. And there he remained throughout the night. In the morning, Jesus called twelve particular disciples to him and he named them 'apostles'. He was anointing them with specific power so that he could train them and eventually send them forth to preach, heal, and cast out devils; as an extension of himself. And this is where he surnamed Simon 'Peter'. And he surnamed James and John 'Boanerges' (which means, 'sons of Thunder'). Then Jesus came back down from the mountain with his twelve apostles and they stood in the plain — together with the great multitude that had followed along with them. And he began to open his mouth and teach *(this was a sermon that would come to be known as the 'Sermon on the Mount')*. **— (Matt 12:15-21 [& 5:1-2] & Mark 3:7-19 & Luke 6:12-19)**

Jesus began; "Blessed are the poor in spirit: for theirs is the Kingdom of Heaven. Blessed are they that mourn; for they shall be comforted. Blessed are the meek; for they shall inherit the earth. Blessed are they which do hunger and thirst after righteousness; for they shall be filled. Blessed are the merciful; for they shall obtain mercy. Blessed are the pure in heart; for they shall see God. Blessed are the peacemakers: for they shall be called the children of God. Blessed are they which are persecuted for righteousness' sake; for theirs is the Kingdom of Heaven. Blessed are ye when men shall hate you and persecute you and say all manner of evil against you, falsely, for my sake. Rejoice, and be exceeding glad — for great is your reward in heaven; for so persecuted they the prophets which were before you. But woe to you that are rich; for you have received your consolation already. Woe to you that are full; for you shall yet hunger. Woe to you that laugh now; for you will mourn and weep later. Woe to you, when all men shall speak well of you; for so did their fathers to the false prophets." — *(Matt 5:3-12 & Luke 6:20-26)*

And Jesus continued teaching his disciples, there in the plain — saying; "You are the salt of the earth; to season each other. If you have no saltiness to enhance each other with, you are of no use to God. You are also the light of the world, and you have not been lighted so that you could hide under a table; but a light that is held up high gives light to the whole house. *(We are 'saved' for the purpose of serving God and His Kingdom.)* Let your light so shine before men, that when they see good works performed through you, they will glorify God *(not you)*. I have not come to destroy the law or the prophets *(the Old Testament truths)* I am come to fulfill them. For, Here is truth:

until heaven and earth pass away, nothing shall be taken away from the law or prophecy until all is fulfilled. Anyone who breaks any of these commandments — or, teaches men to break them — will be called the least in the Kingdom of Heaven. But whoever obeys and teaches my commandments will be called great in the Kingdom of Heaven. And unless your righteousness exceed the righteousness of the Lawyers and Pharisees of Israel, you will not enter into the Kingdom of Heaven." *(This was true, because the Lawyers and Pharisees of Israel did not retain any further Word from God beyond the first-half of His 'amendment' to mankind [the Old Testament Law]; they stubbornly refused to accept the last half of God's amendment [the Gospel of the New Testament]. The first half of God's amendment strengthens and restores a right mind and will, in a man — but the last half, strengthens and restores a right heart. Without the last half of God's amendment, a man cannot enter into the Kingdom of Heaven.)* **— (Matt 5:13-20)**

And Jesus began to teach the commandments of God to his disciples in a more excellent way; through their hearts. Among many other things, he taught them that there are many different ways to 'slay' your brother *(besides physically murdering him)* — and we are equally accountable for all of them. — *(Matt 5:21-22)*

He also taught them that a 'good' work cannot be performed through a man while his conscience is not clean before God. — *(Matt 5:23-24)*

And; that we will always come out ahead if we try to make peace with each other, rather than taking each other to court *(because court will always cost us more than we bargained to pay)*. — *(Matt 5:25-26)*

And Jesus taught them that a man is guilty of adultery (in God's eyes) the moment his mind agrees to engage in it *(because that is the point at which the 'seed' of sin has been embraced and planted)*. — *(Matt 5:27-28)*

And he emphasized that damage to our spirit is far more harmful to us than damage to our body. — *(Matt 5:29-30)*

He taught them that the only justifiable grounds for divorce (in God's eyes) is adultery. — *(Matt 5:31-32)*

And; that when a man swears an oath, it amounts to sinful boasting (in God's eyes). - *(Matt 5:33-37)*

Jesus taught them that every man is called to 'bear' loss and assault, rather than to resist them *(perhaps because earthly issues are far less important than the eternal condition of the souls involved in the squabble)*. - *(Matt 5:38-39 & Luke 6:29-30)*

He also said that whatever someone asks of us, we must give it (if we have it, to give). - *(Matt 5:40-42)*

And; that we are called to love all men — friend or enemy — and pray for them *(demonstrating the 'image/likeness of God')*. - *(Matt 5:43-48)*

He taught them that as God's children, we are called to do 'good' to those who hate us and to bless those who offend us. — *(Luke 6:27-28)*

And; that we should treat people the way we'd like them to treat us; being merciful in all things. — *(Luke 6:31-36)*

Jesus also taught them that if a man gives a charitable gift — hoping to be noticed by men — he will receive no reward from God. - *(Matt 6:1-4)*

Likewise; that if a man prays — hoping to be noticed by men — his prayer will not be honored by God. — *(Matt 6:5-13)*

And he taught them that God will only forgive a man of his sins if that man is willing to forgive his own offenders. — *(Matt 6:14-15)*

And Jesus told them that if a man goes on a fast — hoping to be noticed by men — his fast will not be honored by God. — *(Matt 6:16-18)*

And; that every treasure we store up on earth will decay — but treasures we store up in heaven will not decay. — *(Matt 6:19-21)*

And he explained that whatever a man chooses to 'look at' is what will fill him with darkness, or light. — *(Matt 6:22-23)*

And Jesus made it very clear to his listeners that a man either serves God, or he serves Satan (by default). And he stressed the importance of choosing to serve spiritual things rather than physical things — trusting God to provide the latter. — *(Matt 6:24-34)*

He told them that as God's children; we are called to heal each other — not judge and condemn each other. — *(Matt 7:1-5 & Luke 6:39-42)*

Also; that it's not our calling to force-feed his *Word* to rebellious mankind. — *(Matt 7:6)*

Then Jesus assured his followers that if we ask God for provision, he will give it *(and that we will harvest according to what we have planted)*. — *(Matt 7:7-12 & Luke 6:37-38)*

And he explained to them that mankind has hypothesized many paths to God — but God provided only one path; Jesus. — *(Matt 7:13-14)*

He taught them that you can recognize a false prophet by the fruit that he bares; if a man bares bad fruit, he is a bad prophet. — *(Matt 7:15-20)*

And he told them that God 'knows' us when the Holy Spirit of Truth lives in us and 'manifests' through us. If we never receive the Holy Ghost and allow Him to work through us, we have rebelled against God's will. — *(Matt 7:21-23)*

In closing, Jesus told his followers that whoever hears his words and clings to them will always build upon a firm foundation. — *(Matt 7:24-27)*

And in the plain below the mountain in Galilee, Jesus taught his disciples how they could distinguish between those who are 'reborn' *(of God's spirit)* and those who are not: He said that a good spirit doesn't produce corrupt fruit *(hate, anger, chaos, hopelessness, evil, harshness, impatience, arrogance & intemperance)*. Nor, does a corrupt spirit produce good fruit *(love, joy, peace, faith, rightness, gentleness, patience, humility & self-control)*. This is true because whatever is in a man's heart is what his mouth will speak. He said that a 'good' man — out of the 'good' treasure of his heart — brings forth things that are good. And he added that you will never see men gleaning fruit from a thorn bush. Jesus went on to explain how ludicrous it is for a man to call him 'Lord' or 'Master', having no intention *(or desire)* to ever 'serve' him. He said; "The man who hears the Word of my Gospel and actually does that which it calls them to do; that man will build upon a solid rock from that point forward. But the man who hears my Word and does not do it; everything he builds will crumble and fall." And when Jesus had finished his teachings, his disciples were astonished at his doctrine; for, he taught them as one having authority — not like the Lawyers. And as he left the mountain, great multitudes followed him. **— (Matt 7:28—8:1 & Luke 6:43-49)**

Upon his return to Capernaum, a man approached Jesus and asked him to heal a certain Roman Centurion's servant (who, was near death with the palsy, some distance away). This Gentile had said to Jesus; "I understand the power of your authority; just speak the Word and my servant shall be healed." And Jesus marveled at the fact that this Gentile had displayed more faith than the nation of Israel. He told the man; "Just as you believe, so let it be done." And the servant was healed in the very moment Jesus spoke the words, aloud. — *(Matt 8:5-13 & Luke 7:1-10)*

The next day, Jesus would go into a city called Nain; he, and many of his disciples and a multitude of followers. And as they approached the city's gate, there was a dead man being carried out; the only son of his mother (who was also a widow). When Jesus saw her, he had compassion on her and he told her; "Do not cry." And he came and touched the dead body of her son and said; "Young man, arise." Therefore, her dead son sat upright and began to speak — and he was returned to his mother. And fear came over everyone who watched. And many people glorified God that day. And it was rumored throughout the lands, thereafter, that God has visited His people. – *(Luke 7:11-17)*

Now, when John the Baptist heard of everything that Jesus did among the people — yet, he himself remained in prison — he sent two of his disciples to ask Jesus; "Are you the Messiah — or should we watch for some other, to come?" *(John — like so many other believers — was frustrated by the nagging question, 'If you are Christ [the 'king'] then why aren't you claiming your throne...and, getting me out of jail, while you're at it?!' John 'knew' that Jesus was the Messiah; he was simply asking for encouragement [in the form of an explanation].)* Now, in that hour Jesus had healed and cleansed many folk in the area. Therefore, he told John's disciples; "Go and tell John everything that you have seen and heard, yourselves; that I am making people whole, preaching the Gospel to the poor, raising the dead to life — and blessed is every man who does not rebel against me." *(Jesus was reminding John that he was still about the business of performing all the specific 'activities' that God had foretold Israel the Messiah would perform when he arrived. He was providing John a reason to remain patient.) - (Matt 11:2-6 & Luke 7:18-23)*

And after John's disciples had departed back to the prison, Jesus began to teach the people regarding John. He asked them; when they first heard of John *(preaching 'repent and be baptized')*, what was it that drew them to go out and listen to John? Was it an entertaining show that they sought? Or, were they hoping to hear God speak to them again, through a true prophet? And answering his own question, Jesus said; "Yes, and I tell you, he was much more than just a prophet; he was the greatest prophet ever born of a woman." He explained that God himself had sent John, as a messenger; to prepare the way for the Messiah *(just as God had sent prophecy to prepare the way before truth)*. "But," he said, "The Son of man is greater than John." *(In other words; he was expressing that the 'manifestation' itself is greater than the prophecy of it.)* 'Prophecy' was in fact 'Elias' *(which, was prophesied to precede the arrival of the Messiah)*. Now, everyone in the crowd who had been water-baptized *(of John's baptism)* understood Jesus' Words, and justified God. But all of the Pharisees and

Lawyers of Israel *(people who had never repented and been water-baptized)* were unable to receive Jesus' Words (because they remained blind). *(Until a man repents and becomes willing to surrender his earthly being to God's will, he will remain blind.)* Therefore, they rejected everything Jesus had to say. These, had first condemned the solitary John (who, lived in the desert, eating only locusts and honey) — and later, they condemned Jesus (who did the exact opposite; feasting and mingling with the multitudes); they accused both men of being instruments of the Devil. But the wisdom that a man is willing to receive is the wisdom his attitude will reveal; either the inferior wisdom of the world, or the more excellent wisdom of God. It's each man's choice. — *(Matt 11:7-19 & Luke 7:24-35)*

And then Jesus went on to make an example of the cities to whom he had preached the Gospel of peace — which yet rejected him. He wanted to make the point that it would be more tolerable for the cities of Sodom and Gomorrah, in the end time, than for these cities — because these cities had been given the benefit of the Gospel enlightenment (which had never been made available to Sodom and Gomorrah), and still they rejected him. Jesus went as far as to pray to God out loud; thanking God for hiding His wisdom from those who are content with worldly wisdom. And he told the crowds that no man would ever be able to discover 'truth' except through him. Then, he appealed to the Lost Sheep in the crowd, saying; "Come to me, all of you who labor under the weight of this world; and I will give you rest." Jesus urged them that if they would accept him and learn about him, they would find that he is a gentle master — and they would finally have rest for their souls. *(The burden of service to Jesus is simply to love.)* — **(Matt 11:20-30)**

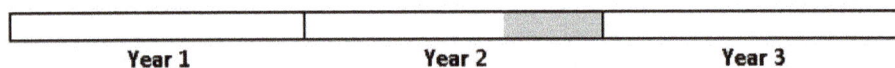

Year 1	**Year 2**		**Year 3**

And one of the Pharisees of Israel (named Simon) asked Jesus to come and eat with him. And so, they went to his home. *(And they happened to be in the vicinity of Magdala, at this time [Matt 15:39].)* And as they sat down to eat, a woman (who was in the city) came into the house — bringing with her an alabaster box of ointment *(which, was very expensive).* *(Later [in John 11:2] we will be told, plainly, that this woman was Mary [the Magdalene].)* Having entered the house, Mary *(who, was a sinner having seven devils)* went directly to Jesus and knelt down at his feet, crying. And as her tears dropped upon his feet, she wiped them away again with her own hair. And she began to kiss Jesus' feet repeatedly, as she anointed them with the precious ointment from her alabaster box. Now, when Jesus knew that his host began to question *(in his mind)* why Jesus allowed this 'unclean' woman to touch him, Jesus turned to the man and asked, "Simon; If a man forgives the debts owed to him by two friends — one friend owing more than the other — which friend would be the most grateful?" And Simon answered him; "I suppose the friend he forgave the greatest debt." Jesus said; "That's right. This woman before me has washed and dried and anointed my feet with ointment — and she has not stopped kissing my feet since she arrived. You have offered me no such kindness. She has gratefully received forgiveness for many sins, being full of love — but to those who love little, little is forgiven." And he said to Mary; "Your faith has saved you. Go in peace." *(Every time I read this passage, the same thought occurs to me: Why* *on earth would an important Pharisee allow a known, sinful woman to waltz right into his home and approach one of his guests in such an intimate manner? Is it possible that Simon the Pharisee may have been Mary's father? We know that she was wealthy, by the gift with which she anointed Jesus' feet. The possibility of this scenario occurs to me for several reasons. At the end of Jesus' ministry, the scripture tells us Jesus spends all of crucifixion week lodging in the home of Simon the Leper [Mark 14:3} — which appears to be the same home that Mary and Martha and Lazarus shared [Luke 10:38 & John 12:1-2]. What if Simon the Pharisee were the father of Mary and Martha and Lazarus — and at some point during Jesus' ministry, he contracted leprosy and moved to Bethany to live with his children [becoming Simon the Leper]? This course of events might even explain the apparently sudden wealth of the rich young ruler [Lazarus] and his youthful pliability with regard to Jesus' guidance and wisdom. These are, of course, only my personal thoughts.) — (**Luke 7:36-50**)*

Afterward, Jesus went throughout every city and village, preaching and showing the 'good' tidings of the Kingdom of God; and the Twelve Apostles were with him, learning and growing in their anointing. As were certain women Jesus had healed and cleansed — such as Mary (the Magdalene) (from whom, he had cast out seven devils) and many others who made provision for Jesus out of their own substance, during his ministry. — *(Luke 8:1-3)*

And coming together among the multitudes again, Jesus cast out an unclean spirit from a deaf and dumb man — at which opportunity, the Lawyers and Pharisees of Israel began to accuse Jesus of casting out devils by the power of Satan. But Jesus immediately pointed out to them that a house divided against itself will fall — so, what purpose would it serve for the Devil to actively fight against himself? He added, that on the other hand; if the Devil is being effectively cast out of people (by Jesus' hand), then the Kingdom of God must truly have arrived; because, only God is able to bind the Devil and cast him out. Then Jesus explained to them that after the Holy Spirit casts the Devil out of a soul *(cleansing that vessel)*, that soul becomes eligible to invite Christ *(the seed of the Holy Spirit of Truth; the bridegroom)* inside. But if that soul does not invite Christ into his heart *(out loud)*, he automatically remains against Christ (by default). Furthermore; Jesus told them that all sins will be forgiven of men (every possible sin) — except for blaspheming against the Holy Spirit of Truth *(by counting the Holy Spirit as evil or, powerless or, worthless)* — that particular sin will never be forgiven; not on earth, nor, in heaven. Jesus explained this in detail because the Pharisees had just called the power inside of him 'the Devil'. *(They had just blasphemed the Holy Spirit of Truth.)* — **(Matt 12:22-37 & Mark 3:20-30)**

With that, the Pharisees of Israel demanded to see a sign from Jesus. But Jesus told them he would not provide them any new sign. He told them the only sign they would get was the Old Testament account of Jonah and the whale — and, that just like Jonah, the Son of man would spend three days and nights in the heart of the earth. And he added, that not even this event would be enough to melt the hardness of their hearts. Then Jesus explained to them that when a Devil is cast out of a man (by Holy Spirit), it immediately goes around looking for a new home. And when it can't find a new home it tries to return to its former home (taking along seven other devils, for reinforcement). And when it finds its former home empty *(cleaned and swept, but not occupied by a new 'master')* — then, all those devils move into that soul; and the end-state of that soul is worse than it was in the beginning. Jesus told the crowds that this will be the case for every man who has been cleansed and reclaimed by God *(repented, and been water-baptized)*, only to refuse to accept the Son of man *(into his heart)* as his new master *(by obeying his command to 'serve' God, with him)*. – ***(Matt 12:38-50 & Mark 3:31-35)***

The same day, Jesus went again to the shore of the Sea of Galilee, and boarded a ship (from which, he spoke to the great multitudes who had gathered on the shore, to hear him). He spoke many things to them, in parables (stories; that only repentant souls could understand). He spoke of a farmer who planted seeds in various different places; planting some on thoroughfares, where birds came and ate the seeds. And planting some in rocky places, where they were easily burnt up by the sun. And planting some among thornbeds, where they were choked out by growing weeds. And planting some on rich, fertile soil, where they were able to flourish and produce various amounts of fruit. At a later time, Jesus will explain to his disciples, privately, that people who aren't really seeking the truth and wisdom of God *(in other words; God's will)* will never be able to make sense of the Gospel Jesus preaches *(the New Testament Word)*. But that he, himself *(Christ; the seed of Holy Spirit of Truth; the bridegroom)* will personally explain God's truths to every man who is truly willing to worship God *(in truth and love)*. He will also tell them *(at that later time)* that the more they learn and understand of him, the more they'll be able to further learn and understand *(in other words; the anointed Word increases our power to understand the thoughts of God)*. - ***(Matt 13:1-17 & Mark 4:1-13 & Luke 8:4-10)***

At that later time, he will explain the parable of the farmer to his disciples in depth; explaining that the 'seed' is the Word of God. And therefore; the seed which was planted on the thoroughfares represents Word that lands in the ears of people who are bustling about with the cares of this world *(people who are too distracted to acknowledge it)*. When that seed falls, it is simply snatched away again, by the Devil. And the seed which was planted in rocky places represents Word that lands in the ears of people who like the sound of it — but they have no 'good master' *(in their heart)* to translate it into useable wisdom for them. That seed is easily forsaken the first time it causes a ripple in their life instead of a cure. And the seed which was planted among thornbeds represents Word that lands in the ears of people who like the sound of it — but they aren't willing to trade in their sinful lifestyle, in return. That seed is quickly discarded when they realize they can't have both. And the seed which was planted in the rich, fertile soil represents Word that lands in the ears of people who like the sound of it, and also have Jesus in their heart *(to translate the wisdom of it)*, and are also willing to trade their worldly pursuits for the opportunity to pass on the good news they have received *(rightly discerning that a candle is 'lighted' in order to 'give light')*. Jesus will tell his disciples *(at that later time)* that they will plant the seeds of his Word hereafter, and Heaven will bring the increase. *(This is a very important passage. This is where we learn that it is not our job to convert a lost soul to Christ; our job is to drop the seeds into their souls [the Word, the love, the goodness, the forgiveness, etc...]. It is the Holy Spirit's job to 'convert' the soul. Often, when we toil relentlessly on a particular soul, to no avail, we're tempted to think there's something wrong with our own faith or effort. Nothing could be farther from the truth. Some souls simply can't be saved — and God knows who they are.)* **— (Matt 13:18-23 & Mark 4:14-29 & Luke 8:11-18)**

In any event; for now, Jesus remained on the boat (on the shore of the Sea of Galilee) telling the crowds many other parables about the Kingdom of Heaven. He told them that the kingdom is like a farmer who planted good seed in his fields one day, and then went to bed. And while he slept, his enemy came and planted thorn bushes among his wheat. And when the thorns and the wheat began to grow together, the farmer couldn't pull out the thorns without damaging the wheat — so, he had to leave them both to grow together until the harvest. And at harvest time the reapers would gather the thorns and burn them up. Also, he told them the kingdom is like a farmer who planted a mustard seed — which is the smallest of all seeds — but when the plant becomes full grown, it shoots out great branches — becoming a tree that lodges many birds. Also, he said the Kingdom of Heaven is like a woman who put some leaven into a little flour, and the leaven grew to permeate the whole batch of bread dough *(the 'life' of it, growing into its fullness)*. Just then, Jesus' mother and brothers arrived among the crowd; passing word through to Jesus that they wanted to speak to him. And when the message was repeated aloud to Jesus, he took the opportunity to teach the crowd that, in fact; every soul who performs the will of God is Jesus' 'brother', 'sister' and 'mother'. — *(Matt 13:24-35 & Mark 4:30-34 & Luke 8:19-21)*

And when Jesus had finished telling these parables, he sent the multitudes away, and began to edify his parables to his disciples. He said; "He that planted the seed is the Son of man. The 'field' is the world. And the 'good seed' are the children of the kingdom. But the 'thorn bushes' are the children of the Devil. And the 'enemy' that planted the thorns, is the Devil. The 'harvest' is the end of the world, and the 'reapers' are the angels. At the end of this world, the wicked ones will be gathered and burned; then, the righteous will shine forth as the sun in the Kingdom of their Father." Again, Jesus explained that the Kingdom of Heaven is like a precious treasure hidden in a field, which — when a man has found it — he is willing to sell all that he has, just to buy that field. And it's like finding a perfect pearl and then selling everything you have, just to buy it. And it's like a fisherman casting his net into the sea, and drawing it up full — then separating the good fish from the bad. Then Jesus asked his disciples if they understood everything he had taught them, and they said; "Yes, Lord." And Jesus said; "Every Scribe *(of God's Word)* is like a homeowner who brings forth from his house both old treasures and new treasures—(i.e.; He must faithfully proclaim both the Old Testament Word, and the New Testament Word)." — *(Matt 13:36-53)*

And when evening was come, they passed over the Sea of Galilee; they, and other ships. And there arose a great windstorm that caused the waves to fill the ship — and his disciples were afraid. And Jesus (sleeping peacefully on his pillow) they woke up, to save them. And Jesus rebuked the wind, saying; "Peace; be still." And immediately the wind ceased. And Jesus said to them; "How is it that you have no faith?" And they were astounded that even the wind and sea obeyed Jesus. - *(Matt 8:18-27 & Mark 4:35-41 & Luke 8:22-25)*

And when they landed on shore in the land of the Gadarenes and Gergesenes, two possessed men ran out of the tombs — and one of them ran to Jesus. Jesus said to the man; "Come out of him, unclean spirit." And the unclean spirit replied; "Torment me not, Son of the most high God." And Jesus asked him; "What is your name?" And the unclean spirit replied; "My name is Legion; for we are many." And the devils asked Jesus not to cast them out into the deep — but rather; to send them into a great heard of pigs that was nearby. Jesus gave them leave, and the devils left the man and entered into the swine (which, then ran violently down a steep hill, into the sea, and drowned). And the people of that land asked Jesus to leave, because they were taken with great fear. - *(Matt 8:28-34 & Mark 5:1-20 & Luke 8:26-39)*

And when they had passed back over again *(to the other side of the Sea of Galilee)*, many people gathered around them, again. And there came to Jesus one of the rulers of the Synagogue, named Jairus. He fell down at Jesus' feet and begged him to come lay his hands upon his daughter (who was sick to the point of death); so that she may live. And as Jesus walked through the crowd with the man *(toward his house)*, he suddenly felt virtue escape from his body. Knowing that someone *(of faith)* had touched his clothes and been healed by it, Jesus stopped and turned around sharply, asking; "Who touched my clothes?" And a woman came out from the crowd and fell down before Jesus, trembling in fear. This woman had a blood disease and had suffered many things of many doctors, for twelve years — yet, she remained uncured. Aware of the many miracles accounted to Jesus, she had crept up to him from behind to touch his garment — because she believed that if she simply touched his clothing, she would be healed *(and indeed, she was)*. So, she fell down before Jesus, and told him the truth. And Jesus said to her; "Daughter, your faith has healed you. Go in peace." **- *(Matt 9:18-22 & Mark 5:21-34 & Luke 8:40-48)***

And while Jesus had been distracted with this woman and her plague, the daughter of Jairus succumbed to her illness and passed away. And a messenger appeared and reported it to Jesus, just then. Nevertheless, Jesus told the ruler; "She is not dead; she only sleeps. Hold fast your faith." And they continued on, to his house. Approaching the child's bedside with only her parents and Peter, James & John; Jesus took the girl by the hand and said to her; "Maid, arise." With that, the child immediately responded; rising and walking (for, she was 12-years-old). *(Once again; the age of twelve is noted to have been the age at which a person begins to be able to hear the voice of God; as suggested earlier in the case of the twelve year-old Jesus, as well as with young Samuel [the prophet of the Old Testament].)* — **(Matt 9:23-26 & Mark 5:35-43 & Luke 8:49-56)**

And as Jesus departed from the house of Jairus afterward, two blind men followed him — begging him to have mercy on them and to heal them. And Jesus asked them; "Do you believe that I am able to heal you?" And they said; "Yes, Lord." Then Jesus touched their eyes and said; "According to your faith, let it be so done to you." And their sight was restored to them. And just as he had on many other occasions of healing or cleansing, Jesus instructed these men; "Do not tell men what I have done for you." *(This; because Jesus didn't want the whole world to know he was Christ until after he was killed and resurrected. Otherwise; some, might have tried to prevent his crucifixion.)* Unfortunately, these men were unable to keep their joy contained, and the fame of Jesus continued to spread abroad, anyway. — *(Matt 9:27-34)*

Then Jesus returned, once again, to Nazareth *(his own country)*. And he began again to teach in the Synagogue, on the weekly Sabbaths. But the humanness of Jesus was still so real to these *(these, who had grown up alongside of the 'man')* that very few were able to stretch their minds beyond his skin and bones to accept the presence of God within him. Therefore, Jesus could still do very little healing among those of Nazareth. And, again he marveled at their lack of faith (after everything they had witnessed of him). — *(Matt 13:54-58 & Mark 6:1-6)*

And Jesus continued to go about the cities and villages of Galilee, teaching in their Synagogues —

preaching the kingdom, and healing and cleansing. And as Jesus watched the multitudes that followed after him, he was moved with compassion toward them — for, they followed and listened (and fainted) and were scattered abroad like sheep with no shepherd. So, Jesus mentioned to his disciples that the harvest looks great, but the gardeners are few. And he asked his disciples to pray to God that He would send laborers into the field. — *(Matt 9:35-38)*

Then Jesus called together the Twelve Apostles *(whom he had anointed earlier for learning and preaching)*, and he anointed them again; this time, with power and authority over all devils (because he was now ready to send them out into the land, as an extension of himself; to heal the sick, cast out devils, raise the dead and preach the Kingdom of God). *(Bear in mind that these Twelve Apostles had not yet received the 'full' baptism of the Holy Ghost; nevertheless, God was able to use them [and called them, for use] even as their full sanctification was still in progress.)* And Jesus paired the apostles in twos, and told them to put on their shoes and coats, grab their staffs, and take no other provision with them. And he commanded them to go and seek out all those who are circumcised and preserve the commandments of God—(i.e.; those repentant, and obedient to the Old Testament), to tell them the Kingdom of God has arrived. *(Jesus was sending the Twelve Apostles to the 'Lost Sheep of Israel' [whom God had 'prepared' — through the Old Testament Word and through water-baptism — to receive Christ when he manifested].)* And (because prepared-Israel was intended to receive Christ, first) Jesus gave them this instruction; "Do not go into the land of the (unprepared) Gentiles and Samaritans. And when you first enter a town of Israel, ask to be directed to the home of someone who is worthy to receive the Holy Spirit *(someone who has repented and been water-baptized according to John's message)* — and if in fact they are worthy, let your peace [Holy Spirit] come upon that house. And lodge there until you move on. And whoever refuses to receive you — or, the Word of the Lord — shake the dust of them off your feet and continue on your way." *(Later; Jesus would also add; "And in the same house remain; do not go from house to*

house [Luke 10:7].") — *(**Matt 10:1-14 & Mark 6:7-11 &
Luke 9:1-5)***

And Jesus explained to his Twelve Apostles that
he was sending them out like sheep among wolves — and
therefore; they should be as wise as serpents, and
yet, as harmless as doves. *(In other words; Jesus was
telling them to be committed to both the Old and New
Testaments; to honor the Law and promises [of Old
Testament prophecy] as well as to trust in the 'self-
sacrificing' method [of ministry] that he, himself,
was setting as an example for them [in the New
Testament].)* Jesus warned them to beware of men
because they were going to be hated and abused all
along the way, for proclaiming his message. Jesus told
them not to worry over what to say when those times
come — because the Holy Spirit would speak through
them in those moments. He told his Twelve brave
Apostles that when men persecute them in one city,
they should just flee to some other city — because
there is plenty of ground to cover. He explained that
it's now their ongoing job (until the Son of man
returns) to walk the same path they see Jesus walking,
on earth — which, is a path of self-sacrifice. He told

them to preach what they hear from him, and not fear those who can only harm their physical body — but rather, to fear God (who can destroy their body and their soul). And he told them to take comfort in knowing that God is in full control of every moment of the life that is devoted to Him. He explained to his Twelve Apostles that any man who believes and accepts him becomes part of him (and part of his Father) and, by default, is put at odds with their own loved ones who are still part of the world. He told them that no man can be part of both the Father and the world — and whatever they're willing to put into their relationship with God is exactly what they'll get back out of it. With that, the Twelve Apostles were dispatched into all the land (to represent Jesus in the world; healing and preaching and casting out devils). — *(Matt 10:15—11:1 & Mark 6:12-13 & Luke 9:6)*

Now, Herod (the Jewish Tetrarch) had laid hold on John the Baptist some time earlier, and imprisoned him (because John had rebuked Herod, for taking his own brother's wife). And as John lingered in Herod's jail, it came to pass one day that Herod's own pride had recklessly resulted in the beheading of John. And in that day, the Twelve Apostles happened to be returning (to Jesus) from their ministry exploits, abroad — when they crossed paths with John's disciples (who, had just collected John's body, and buried it). Having nowhere else to go, now, John's disciples decided to return to Jesus with the Twelve Apostles. When the apostles were finished giving Jesus a full report of all that had transpired (both; with them, and with John and his disciples), they departed together by ship to a desert place in Bethsaida, where they might rest themselves. Nevertheless; when the multitudes heard of it they followed after them, from every city. — *(Matt 14:1-13 & Mark 6:14-33 & Luke 9:7-10 & John 6:2-3)*

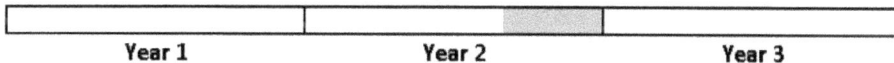

Year 1	Year 2	Year 3

And in the desert — as Jesus looked out upon the multitudes that followed him — his compassion for them grew. For, even as the Feast of the Passover was now at hand, still they followed Jesus (into a desert place). *(And this was, now, the second Passover event, since the beginning of Jesus' salvation ministry; it was the end of the second year of his ministry.)*

Overcome with compassion for the multitude, Jesus instructed Philip and Andrew and the other disciples to feed this crowd of more than five thousand souls (having only five loaves of bread and two fish). And when they had brought the available bread and fish to Jesus, he took them into his own hands and (lifting them up) gave thanks; blessing them — and broke them. Then, he put the food back into the hands of his disciples (to feed the multitudes with them). And the entire crowd was filled; leaving twelve baskets of fragments, remaining. — *(Matt 14:14-21 & Mark 6:34-44 & Luke 9:11-17 & John 6:4-13)*

And when the multitudes witnessed this miracle, they said to each other that Jesus was truly the Messiah. And when Jesus perceived that the crowd was about to take him by force (to set him as 'king'), he sent the multitudes away and commanded his disciples to take ship back across the sea (toward Capernaum) — although, he himself went up into the mountain to pray. Several hours later (somewhere between 3:00 and 6:00 a.m.); as the disciples struggled vigorously against a windstorm on the sea, Jesus saw them struggling — and he went to them, walking upon the water. And when the disciples saw a man walking toward them (on top of the water) the sight frightened them. But Jesus called out to them; "Do not be afraid — it is I." And Peter said to him; "If it is you, master, bid me come to you upon the water." And so, Jesus said; "Come." And as Peter walked upon the water, toward Jesus, the winds kicked up and frightened Peter and he immediately began to sink. But he called out to Jesus; "Lord, save me!" And Jesus immediately stretched forth his hand and caught him. And again, Jesus marveled at their lack of faith; for they had already forgotten the power behind the miracle of the loaves and fishes. Nevertheless; when they climbed back onto the boat, the winds stopped and they told Jesus; "Truly, you are the Son of God." And the ship was immediately on the shore of Gennesaret. And the people of that land knew of Jesus and immediately began to rush around (bringing him their diseased and possessed). — *(Matt 14:22-36 & Mark 6:45-56 & John 6:14-21)*

On the following day — when the multitudes could not find Jesus — they also took ship, sailing to Capernaum (hoping that Jesus would be meeting up with his disciples, there). And when the multitudes found Jesus on the other side of the sea, Jesus said to them; "Here is truth: you don't seek me because of the miracles you saw me perform — but rather; because when you ate the loaves, you were filled. I tell you, labor not for meat that perishes — but rather; for that meat which remains eternally (which, the Son of man shall give you — for, he has God sealed)." Then the multitudes asked him; "What shall we do to work the works of God?" And Jesus answered; "This is the work of God; that you believe on the one (Jesus) He has sent to save you." They asked; "What can you show us that would help us believe? Our Fathers were fed manna, in the desert; from heaven *(as a sign)*." But Jesus answered them; "Here is truth: Moses did not give you that bread which is from heaven. But my Father gives you the true bread from heaven. For, the true bread of God is He (Jesus) who comes down from Heaven and restores life to the world." And the multitudes said; "Lord, give us this bread for evermore *(the Word of the Gospel)*." — *(John 6:22-34)*

And so, Jesus continued feeding his sheep, saying; "I am the bread of life. Whoever comes to me shall never hunger — and whoever believes on me shall never thirst *(for Holy Spirit)*. But I have said that you have seen me and do not believe. Everyone that the Father *(Goodness & Truth, the Father)* gives me, will come to me. And whoever comes to me *(Goodness & Truth, the Son)*, I will no way cast out. For, I came down from heaven to do the will of He who sent me. And this is His will; that of every soul which He *(Goodness & Truth, the Father)* has given me, I should lose no one; but raise them all up again, in the last day — that everyone who sees the Son *(Goodness & Truth, the Son)* and believes on him *(loves and obeys him)*, may have eternal life. And I will raise him up at the last day." — *(John 6:35-40)*

And the Jews among the crowd began to murmur at Jesus, because he said; "I am the bread which came down from heaven." Jesus was the Son of a lowly carpenter from Nazareth *(a fact well known, to the Jews)* — yet, Jesus claimed to have come down from heaven. This caused great bitterness in the Jews. But Jesus said to them; "Don't murmur among yourselves; no one is able to come to me *(Goodness & Truth, the Son)* unless God *(Goodness & Truth, the Father)* draws him to me — and I will raise that one up *(the lover of Truth & Goodness)* at the last day. It was provided in the Old Testament scriptures that they shall all be taught of God *(Goodness & Truth, the Father)* — and every man who has heard and learned of the Father *(through the Old Testament Word)*, will eventually recognize and be drawn to me *(Goodness & Truth, the Son)*. Here is truth: he that believes on me has eternal life; I am the bread of *(eternal)* life. Your Fathers were fed manna in the wilderness — yet, they are dead. I am the bread that a man may eat, and never die. I am the living *(eternal)* bread — and the bread that I will give is my own flesh *(my willing sacrifice)*, which I will give for the life of the world." **- *(John 6:41-51)***

Then the Jews strove among themselves, debating how Jesus could give them his flesh to eat. Again, Jesus said; "Here is truth: If you do not eat the flesh of the Son *(the Word of the Gospel)*, and drink in his blood *(Holy Spirit)*, you have no *(eternal)* life in you. For, my flesh is meat, indeed — and my blood is drink, indeed." *(The physical body requires physical 'food', to live and grow. The mind requires 'knowledge', to live and grow. The restored heart requires the 'Word of God', to live and grow.)* Jesus went on, to say; "He who eats my flesh *(the Word)* and drinks in my blood *(Holy Spirit)* dwells in me — and I, in him. As the living Father has sent me, and I live by the Father — so then, whoever eats me *(the Word)* shall live by me." These things, Jesus said, in the Synagogue as he taught in Capernaum, near Gennesaret. But many of Jesus' own disciples murmured at this saying; because it was so hard to understand. So, Jesus said to them; "What if you see the Son of man ascending back up into heaven? You would see that it is the spirit that ascends; the flesh profits nothing. The Words that I speak to you are spiritual *(Goodness & Truth)*, and they are *(eternal)* life. But some of you don't believe the Spirit of my Words *(the Spirit of Truth)* — that was why I told you that no man can come to me unless the Holy Spirit *(of Truth)* draws *(attracts)* him to me." With that, many of Jesus' own disciples walked away. Then Jesus said to his Twelve Apostles; "Will you also walk away?" And Simon (Peter) answered him; "Lord, to whom shall we go? You have the Words of eternal life. We believe and are sure you are the Christ *(the seed of Holy Spirit of Truth)*; the Son of God *(Holy Spirit of Truth)*." So, Jesus made it known to Simon (Peter) that even though He had chosen *(and ordained)* each one of the Twelve Apostles — nevertheless, one of them is a devil (who will eventually betray him). — *(John 6:52-71)*

And it came to pass, that many Pharisees and Lawyers of Israel came to Capernaum to listen to Jesus speak. And they observed that Jesus' disciples ate bread without washing their hands first *(a custom that Jewish Elders had written into their required 'traditions', long ago)*. And they demanded of Jesus to know why his disciples *(Christianized Jews)* did not honor this *(and many other)* Jewish traditions. But Jesus began to rebuke them for all the 'traditions' they have taken it upon themselves to add to the Laws of God — and these, they teach to God's children. Jesus told them they take God's name in vain — honoring Him with their lips, while their hearts are actually far away from His will and commandments; teaching the commandments of men in place of God's commandments. Then Jesus beckoned the attention of the multitudes, and he announced to them; "There is nothing that, entering into a man's mouth, can defile him. Rather, it is what comes out of his mouth that can defile him." And his disciples came to him and asked him to explain this parable. And Jesus said; "Unclean things that go into your mouth and pass through your stomach and get expelled *(as waste)* from your body, haven't entered into your heart. These don't defile you. What defiles a man are the unclean things which come out of his mouth — because, what comes out of your mouth reflects what is in your heart." – *(The corrupt fruit we produce has the power to defile us.)* After this, Jesus could no longer walk in Jewry, because the Jews sought to kill him. **– (Matt 15:1-20 & Mark 7:1-23 & John 7:1)**

And, so; Jesus went into the borders of Tyre and Sidon; away from Galilee. He entered into someone's home *(to rest)*, hoping that no man would know where he was. But Jesus could not be hidden. A young woman recognized him, and came and fell at his feet — and she begged him to cleanse her young daughter of an unclean spirit. The woman was a Gentile *(not a Jew)* and so, Jesus ignored her. But she would not stop crying out to him for help. So, his disciples finally asked Jesus to answer her. Therefore, Jesus began to explain to the woman that it would not be effectual *(would not produce the intended effect)* for him to give the bread of God's 'prepared' children to unprepared dogs. *(Jesus was explaining that the Word/bread [the New Testament Gospel/amendment] could not 'restore' the heart of someone who's mind/will had not already been reformed by the Old Testament/amendment [via repentance and water-baptism].)* And, the Gentile woman responded; "True Lord; but the dogs *(Gentiles)* have eaten the crumbs that fall from the children's *(Jew's)* table." *(In other words — 'We, too, have learned to trust in you; gratefully embracing the Word that Israel has leaked out.')* And in front of his disciples, Jesus said to her; "Oh woman, great is your faith. Let it be as you wish." And her daughter was cleansed the very moment that Jesus spoke the words. — *(Matt 15:21-28 & Mark 7:24-30)*

Then Jesus returned, to the Sea of Galilee. The inhabitants of the lands began again to bring Jesus impotent folk to be healed. And he instructed them to tell no man what miracles he performed on their behalf. But all the more, they published it abroad and were astonished beyond measure. And again Jesus had compassion on the multitudes which followed him. And a second time, he instructed his disciples to feed the crowd (more than 4,000 souls, this time), having only seven loaves of bread and a few fish. Again, Jesus took the bread and fish into his own hands and gave thanks; blessing them, and broke them. And again he put the food back into the hands of his disciples, who fed the multitudes with them. And again, everyone was filled — leaving seven baskets of fragments, remaining. — *(Matt 15:29-38 & Mark 7:31—8:9)*

Then, Jesus took ship and crossed over the Sea of Galilee, landing in the coasts of Dalmanutha (which is Magdala). And immediately the Pharisees of Israel came forth, demanding a sign from Jesus. But Jesus sighed deeply in his spirit — and he asked the Pharisees to go and consider why it is that they seek a 'sign'. *(These Jewish leaders didn't want to accept that it was 'God's will' to open the doors of Heaven to just 'any' human soul who wanted to become a child of God; they coveted the anointing to Israel, alone. Therefore; they would only accept Jesus' at his Word if Jesus forced them to, with proof [via a sign].)*

Jesus told them again that the only sign they need to reflect on is the one that was provided in the story of Jonah *(who, spent three days in the belly of the whale)*. With that, Jesus turned and told his disciples to beware of the leaven of the Pharisees and Herod (the Jewish Tetrarch). But the disciples were still growing in their faith and understanding, and they thought [at first] that Jesus was speaking of food. Eventually, they realized he was talking about the 'doctrine' the Pharisees were teaching to the nation of Israel; referring to it, as 'leaven'. **- (Matt 15:39—16:12 & Mark 8:10-21)**

As Jesus continued to pass from town to town, he came upon a blind man in Bethsaida, and healed him. And traveling onward, they came into the towns of Caesarea Philippi — where they stopped along the way, to pray. And Jesus asked his disciples; "Who do men say that I am?" And they answered; "John the Baptist...or, Elijah...or, some important prophet." And Jesus said; "But who do you think I am?" And Simon (Peter) answered; "You are Christ; the Son of the living God." And Jesus said; "You are very blessed, Simon Barjona; for flesh and blood did not reveal it to you — my Father in heaven *(Goodness & Truth, the Father)*, did. Your name is Peter (which means 'stone'), and upon this rock will I build my church. And the grave shall not prevail against my church. I will give you the keys of the Kingdom of Heaven, and whoever you bind on earth shall be bound in heaven, and whoever you loose on earth shall be loosed in heaven *(remit -vs.- retain; also see John 20:22-23 & Matt 18:18)*." And Jesus charged his disciples, again; "Tell no one that I am the Son of God *(again; because the Son of God had to be successfully crucified as a 'sinner' in order for mankind's debt to be paid)*." — **(Matt 16:13-20 & Mark 8:22-30 & Luke 9:18-21)**

From this time forward, Jesus tried to prepare his disciples for what was to come; how he must go into Jerusalem and be handed over to the Elders and Pharisees of Israel to suffer much torture at their hands — and to be killed, and to be raised from the grave three days later. But his disciples were not able to comprehend what he was saying. *(During Jesus' three year ministry, it never entered the minds of the disciples for a moment that Jesus would [one day] be killed. The disciples all expected Jesus to take the throne of Israel, eventually — [and frankly, no one understood why he delayed doing so]. They didn't want to know what Jesus was talking about when he made statements like the one mentioned in the verse above.)* Peter himself rebuked Jesus, saying; "Never, Lord." But Jesus said to Peter; "Get behind me, Satan." Jesus told Peter that if he valued things of the flesh *(Jesus' bodily life)* above the will of God, then he was an offense to Jesus. Then he called all the people to him, and he told them plainly that anyone who hopes to follow him *(in his earthly mission, and also into eternity)* must be willing not only to let Jesus be taken and killed — but also to willingly give up his own physical life *(just like Jesus)*. And Jesus asked them why on earth they would want to fight for this temporary physical life when he's taught them that they can trade it for a perfect, eternal life in heaven? He also pointed out that no one owns anything valuable enough to trade God for their condemned soul *(when judgment day comes)* — and man is going to face Christ one day, to be judged. Jesus said; "Here is truth: there are some among you who will never taste of death until the Son of man comes in his kingdom *(at the Second Coming)*." — *(Matt 16:21-28 & Mark 8:31—9:1 & Luke 9:22-27)*

And about a week later, Jesus took John and James and Peter up into a high mountain with him, to pray. And as he prayed, his appearance changed; his aura became glistening white. And the glistening apparitions of two other men appeared with him. These three glowing figures discussed the upcoming crucifixion that Jesus must suffer, in Jerusalem. And as they began to talk, Peter and James and John woke up from their sleep. And Peter — presuming the two apparitions to be Moses and Elijah — offered to make tabernacles for all three of them. But while Peter yet spoke, a luminous cloud overshadowed them all. And a voice came out of the cloud, saying; "This is my beloved Son; hear him." And when God had finished speaking, Jesus stood alone; the other two apparitions were no longer separately visible. — *(Matt 17:1-8 & Mark 9:2-8 & Luke 9:28-36)*

And as Jesus came back down the mountain with John and James and Peter, he told them; "Tell this vision to no one until after the Son of man has risen from the dead." And they kept his words — but they wondered what 'risen from the dead' would mean. And, the disciples asked Jesus why the scriptures say that the Messiah won't appear until after Elijah returns — and yet, here he is already. But Jesus explained to them that 'Elijah' is not a person (as they supposed) — but rather; 'Elijah' was the 'prophecy' that would restore all things *(preparing mankind for the Messiah's arrival)*. Jesus said; "Elijah truly has come already. And they didn't recognize him — and they killed him. And the Son of man will suffer likewise, at their hand." Then, the Apostles finally understood that the Spirit of Elijah had indeed already appeared; in John the Baptist *(the prophet who was filled with the Holy Spirit [of Truth] even from his mother's womb)*. − *(Matt 17:9-13 & Mark 9:9-13)*

And returning again to the multitudes below; there came a man who fell at Jesus feet; begging Jesus to heal his son (who was a lunatic). This man had previously asked Jesus' disciples to heal his son — but having tried, the disciples were unable to cast out this particular unclean spirit. So, Jesus responded to the man by re-affirming to him that if he believed, Jesus *(himself)* could heal his son — because

all things are possible to those who believe. And the
man said, crying; "Lord, I believe. Help my unbelief!"
*(The man assumed that the healing hadn't worked
[through the disciples] because his own faith was
somehow lacking.)* Jesus asked the man how long this
spirit had possessed his son. The man answered; "Since
he was a young child." So, Jesus said; "Unclean
spirit; I charge you come out of him — and do not
enter him again." And the unclean spirit threw the boy
to the ground and departed from him; leaving him as
dead. But Jesus took the boy by the hand, and the boy
arose. Afterward, Jesus' disciples came to him and
asked; "Lord, why were we unable to cast out the
Devil?" And Jesus (marveling at how quickly their
faith keeps escaping them) said; "Because of your
unbelief. If you have faith as a mustard seed, you
could say to this mountain 'move', and it would move;
nothing, would be impossible to you. Although; this
kind of spirit can only be cast out by prayer and
fasting." *('This kind of spirit', the verse says.
Clearly, we pick up many undesirable spirits as we
walk this life [simply by agreeing with them in some
sinful deed we perform together]. But what is it that*

can make a particular spirit more deeply-rooted than another; harder to cast out? I believe there is an important reason why. In the above verse, Jesus [first] establishes for us that this spirit has been discernable in the boy from the earliest years of his life. I believe he was making it clear to us that this was an unclean spirit which the boy was born with; a spirit that was passed down to him, through his parents. It makes sense to me that this type of deeply rooted unclean spirit would be much more difficult to separate from a soul. Prayer and Fasting (dining on spiritual nourishment in place of physical nourishment) increases the strength of the 'inner'-man [who, draws nearer to God and His strength, during the fast]. This was the same mechanism Jesus used to strengthen himself during his forty days in the wilderness. No wonder Jesus thought it would be a good idea to shine a spotlight on this subject. Friends; we are not helpless against the powers of darkness! Not even when we are born with them inside of us. A faithful, Godly soul can cast out even the strongest unclean spirit — with the power of Jesus.) — **(Matt 17:14-21 & Mark 9:14-29 & Luke 9:37-43)**

Year 1	Year 2	Year 3

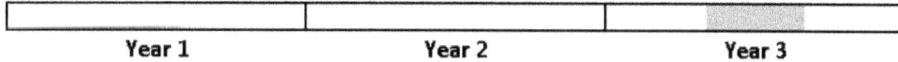

Now, as they travelled from that place, passing through Galilee, Jesus tried again to tell his disciples how he must be delivered into the hands of men...be killed...and be raised from the grave three days later. But still they could not comprehend it — and they were afraid to question him further, about it. And the Jew's Feast of the Tabernacles was nearing. And Jesus' half-brothers began to urge him to go into Judea for the Feast. *(Like so many other men, Jesus' brothers were frustrated by the nagging question, 'If you are Christ [the 'king'], why won't you go and claim your throne?!')*. Jesus answered them, simply; "My time is not yet come. But your time is always ready." He told his half-brothers that the world cannot hate them, because they are still worried about worldly things *(things that have nothing to do with manifesting/replenishing Goodness & Truth in the earth)*. But Jesus the world hates, because Jesus testifies that the works of the world are evil *(works that do not [or, cannot] produce fruit of Goodness/Truth)*. So, Jesus told his brothers to go ahead to the Feast, without him. And they were still in Galilee when they spoke these words to each other. And when Jesus and his disciples were come to Capernaum, some tax collectors approached Peter, and said; "Does your master not pay tribute?" And when Peter moved toward the house to get money for them, Jesus stopped him. He told Peter to go and cast a hook into the sea, and that he would find a piece of money in the mouth of the fish that he would catch. Jesus told Peter to give that money to the tax collector. And Peter did just as Jesus bid him. *(I love this message — 'If you obey me [when I ask you to become fishermen], then I will provide you with whatever things the world demands of you.)* — **(Matt 17:22-27 & Mark 9:30-32 & Luke 9:43-45 & John 7:2-9)**

And when Jesus knew that the disciples had been disputing a certain issue amongst themselves as they travelled, he asked them; "What was it you disputed amongst yourselves?" But they held their peace (for, they had been disputing who is greatest in the Kingdom of Heaven). So, Jesus sat down and called all twelve of the apostles to him. And when he had brought a child into their midst, he told them; "Whoever will humble himself as a little child *(obedient to authority and trusting everything)* he is greatest in the Kingdom of Heaven. Except you be converted and become like a little child, you cannot enter into the Kingdom of Heaven. And anyone who will receive one such converted child in my name, will receive me. And whoever receives me receives not me — but rather; Him that sent me." — *(Matt 18:1-5 & Mark 9:33-37 & Luke 9:46-48)*

Then John told Jesus; "Master, we saw a man casting out devils in your name — but he wasn't one of us, so we forbade him." But Jesus told John; "Do not forbid him. Anyone who is not against us is on our side." *(This is true, because we can only be estranged from Jesus if we 'choose' to be estranged from Jesus.)* Jesus explained to John that any man who is willing to tend Jesus' sheep *(perform the first works; the Good works)* will not lose his reward. *(In these verses, Jesus [himself] is telling his disciples, 'Do not judge and dismiss other workers of Christ just because they aren't on 'exactly' the same page that you are on.' Every time we defame a Catholic...or, a Mormon...or, a Baptist — we are defaming a member of the body of Christ who is struggling in this troubled world to serve God in truth. Tread lightly; Matt 5:22 says; "...whosoever shall say [to a brother/fellow-Christian], Thou fool, shall be in danger of hell fire." It is essential to our joint-mission that we strive to season and encourage one another in a loving and constructive way, because 'a house divided against itself will fall' [Mark 3:25 & Luke 11:17].)* Jesus also told them that any man who offends one of his sheep *(a member of the Body of Christ)* would be better off drowned in the sea. He went as far as to make it clear that (as his little sheep, themselves) if they should ever be unable to control the members of their own body — so as to offend even 'their own' conscience — they would fare better to cut off those unruly members of their own body, than to keep them and risk offending even 'their own' conscience. Afterward, Jesus stressed to his disciples that they have been redeemed in order to save each other *(rather than to condemn each other)*. He said that since it is now their ongoing job to guide and strengthen one another on earth *(spiritually)*; what good would they be, to God, if they fail to enhance and strengthen one

another? Christ had come into the world to save that
which was lost. And thereafter; those souls are being
molded into his image (to carry on his work, when he
leaves). Jesus said; "It is not the will of your
Father in heaven that even one of the sheep *(lovers of
Goodness & Truth)* should perish." — *(Matt 18:6-14 &
Mark 9:38-50 & Luke 9:49-50)*

And Jesus went on; expounding to them that
forgiveness is the 'key'. He explained that, for one
thing; when someone offends you, you should always try
to resolve it right there — between yourself and your
offender. And if your offender refuses to listen to
you (and repent); only then, should you involve a
third witness in the argument. And if even that fails,
they are not to give up on them; then, they should
turn to the church for help with mediation. But Jesus
told them that if their offender remains
unapproachable (and unrepentant) even after all that;
then, they are no longer obligated to forgive the
person. *(Jesus didn't say they 'can't' forgive the
person beyond that point — just, that they are no
longer required to).* Jesus explained again that
whatever they bind on earth shall be bound in heaven —

and whatever they loose on earth, shall be loosed in heaven—*(remit -vs.- retain; also see John 20:22-23 & Matt 16:18-19)*. And he told them; "If two of you (on earth) agree together — as touching anything you ask for — it will be granted by my Father in heaven; because, wherever two or three are gathered together in my name, I am present with them." Then Peter asked Jesus; "How many times must I forgive a brother?" And Jesus replied; "Not just seven times — but rather; seventy times seven." *(In other words; don't put a number on it.)* – **(Matt 18:15-22)**

Then Jesus immediately began to tell them a story of a wicked servant whose king forgave him a great debt that he owed, simply because the servant asked the King for mercy (having no means to pay the debt). Which, same servant — after being released from his debt, by the King — went and found many of his own fellow servants (who, owed him various debts), and he began to choke them and cast them into prison. And when the friends of those servants cried to the King, for help — and when the King realized the cold-heartedness of the servant to whom he had shown mercy — the King called his servant to him and said to him;

"You wicked servant! I forgave you all that debt because you asked for mercy. Shouldn't you have shown the same mercy to your fellow-servants that I showed to you?!" And with that, the King cast him into prison to work off his debt. And Jesus told his disciples; "So, likewise, shall my heavenly Father do also to you, if you refuse to forgive your brothers of their offenses against you." - *(Matt 18:23-35)*

CHAPTER 3 — JESUS RETURNS TO TEACH IN SOUTHERN ISRAEL

Now, the time was drawing near that Jesus should return to Jerusalem to pay the ransom for all mankind. And he set his face toward Jerusalem; sending his messengers before him. And along the way, his disciples entered into a village of the Samaritans to prepare a place for Jesus to overnight, there. But the Samaritans refused to receive Jesus (because he was set on Jerusalem). Therefore; James and John asked Jesus; "Shall we command fire from heaven to come down and consume the Samaritans?" But Jesus answered them; "You don't realize what spirit is in you! The Son of man is not come to destroy men's lives — but rather; to save them!" And as they travelled on, toward another village, a certain Lawyer of Israel approached them and asked Jesus if he could follow him. Jesus told the man that he, himself, had no home and no rest. (The Bible doesn't tell us whether or not that man chose to follow him, thereafter). And another of Jesus own disciples he 'called' to follow him *(in his Good work)* — and that man replied; "Let me first go and bury my Father." But Jesus told him this was his 'call' to preach the Kingdom of God — and to let the dead bury their dead. *(In this verse, I understand Jesus to be relieving this man of all burden relative to his father; no doubt, because the father was a man already eternally estranged from the Kingdom of God, and Jesus knew it [foreknowing all things]. Having no eternal life in him, God and Jesus would consider this man 'dead' [according to Mar 12: 26-67]. Jesus was telling him that at this point, he just needed to obey Jesus; pick up his cross and follow him.)* Then another man volunteered; "Lord, I will follow you; let me just go and say goodbye to my loved ones, first." But Jesus said to him; "No man professing to have chosen the kingdom — but, looking back to worry about worldly things — is fit for the Kingdom of God." *(I've always felt there is an invisible 'yet' at the end of this sentence; that, Jesus is saying — 'If you are still looking back [at worldly things], you're not fully 'committed', yet'.)* — **(Matt 8:19-22 & Luke 9:51-62)**

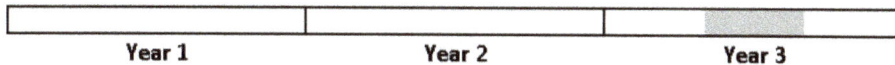

Year 1	Year 2	Year 3

And Jesus and his disciples continued up into Jerusalem, to the Feast of the Tabernacles (albeit, they attended in secret). And the Jews watched for Jesus, there. And many people murmured among the crowds, concerning Jesus. Some thought he was good. Others thought he was deceiving the people. But no one spoke of Jesus openly, for fear of the Jews. And in the midst of the Feast, Jesus went up into the Temple and began to teach. He told the people that the doctrine he teaches came from his Father (who sent him). And that if any man will simply do God's will *(saving that which was lost)*, he will immediately 'know' whether Jesus speaks of his own, or of God's, will. *(How do we answer the rebellious soul who argues that we [Christians] only 'think' we know the truth? I believe the answer to that question lies in the verse above. Its implication is that when a Christian trusts and obeys [willing to perform the Good work] — and the Holy Spirit reciprocates by providing a transformation in that soul [the increase] - then, that transformation/increase is the 'proof'. The end-product of our faithful interaction with God is how we 'know'.)* Jesus went on to tell them; "Anyone who speaks of himself, seeks his own glory. But any man who seeks God's will, is True." He said; "Moses gave you the Law of God *(the Ten Commandments)* — yet, none of you keep it. And you seek to kill me?" — **(John 7:10-20)**

Jesus said; "I do one work; making men 'whole' *(the Good work; the first works)*. And you are offended. If Israel has managed to discern that it's 'good' and 'right' for a man to perform such work as circumcision on the weekly Sabbath day *(whenever the eighth day of life happens to fall on a Sabbath day)* — so that the greater law of Moses isn't broken — why, then, are you scandalized at me for healing a man's withered arm on the Sabbath day?" *(There was one Jewish law that said a baby boy must be circumcised when he is eight days old, or be cast out of Israel. There was another Jewish law that said you can do no work on the Sabbath day. Here, was the conundrum; what happens when a baby boy turns eight days old on the Sabbath day? Should the doctor not perform the work of circumcision? God forbid; the result of that would be much more tragic than simply performing work on a Sabbath day. If Israel was wise enough to weigh out that difficult question of judgment, what was their real problem with Jesus healing a crippled man on the Sabbath day? This was the point Jesus was trying to make to them.)* With that, Jesus told them they need to stop judging by the letter of the law — and rather; weigh things out...to discern the greater good in every situation *(in other words; employing precept upon precept).* And many people in the crowd were amazed that the Jews allowed Jesus to proceed in this manner. And they determined that the Jews must 'know' Jesus is 'Christ'. But some men stumbled on the scriptures (believing no one is supposed to know when Messiah comes). Now, the Jews wanted to overtake Jesus — but his hour had not yet come. Meanwhile, many believed on Jesus, saying; "When Christ comes, will he do more miracles than this man has done?" **— *(John 7:21-31)***

So, when the Pharisees of Israel sent officers to take Jesus by force, Jesus said to the Pharisees; "For a little while longer, I will be with you; then I will return to the one who sent me. And where I go, you will not be able to come." And the Pharisees were confounded by his words. And in the last day of the celebration — that great day of the Feast of the Tabernacles — Jesus stood up and called out to the crowd; "If any man thirst *(for the Holy Spirit of Truth)*, let him come to me and drink. The scripture has promised you that if you believe on me, rivers of living water *(Holy Spirit of Truth)* shall flow out of you." At these words, the people were divided — and even the Roman officers refused to take Jesus by force (as the Pharisees were demanding). The Pharisees said to them; "Are you also deceived by this man? No prophet comes out of Galilee, according to the scripture." Nevertheless; Jesus retired, unscathed, to the Mount of Olives. — *(John 7:32—8:1)*

The next morning, Jesus came again into the Temple to teach — and all the people came to hear him. And as he spoke, the Lawyers and Pharisees of Israel brought before him a woman caught in the act of adultery. They said to Jesus; "The law of Moses commands that this woman be stoned. What do you say?" Jesus stooped down to the ground, and began to write in the dirt *(perhaps, a new law?)*. And when he arose, he answered them; "Let the man who is without sin cast the first stone at her." And something miraculous happened; one by one, the woman's accusers walked away — until only she and Jesus remained. And Jesus said to her; "Woman, where are your accusers? Has no one condemned you?" She answered; "No man, Lord." And Jesus told her; "Nor do I. Go, and sin no more." *(Some theologians speculate this adulterous woman to have been Mary [the Magdalene] — but there is no scripture to support such a theory. The truth is; having been cleansed of all her demons a full year prior to this event [Luke 7:36—8:3], Mary was actually a notoriously beloved and devoted disciple of Jesus, by this time in his ministry.) — **(John 8:2-11)**

Now, when Jesus turned back again, to the people — he told them; "I am the light of the world. He who follows me, will no longer walk in darkness, but shall have the light of life *(Truth; the Holy Spirit)*." And when he said this, the Pharisees of Israel accused

Jesus of being self-professed. But Jesus told them he doesn't bear witness alone; his Father *(who sent him)* also bears witness of him. So, they asked Jesus; "Where is your Father?" And Jesus told them they know neither him, nor his Father. Again, he told them; "I go my way — and where I go, you cannot come." And the Pharisees began to wonder if Jesus planned to kill himself. So, Jesus explained; "You are from beneath — and I am from above. You are of this world — and I am not of this world. You will die in your sin, because you do not believe that I am he *(the Savior promised in Old Testament scripture)*." They said; "Who are you?" Jesus answered; "I am the one *(Goodness & Truth, the Son)* that my Father sent to speak to you the Words that I have heard from Him — and He that sent me is True *(Goodness & Truth, the Father)*." But they did not understand that Jesus spoke of the *(Heavenly)* Father. Jesus told them that once they have 'lifted up' the Son of man, they will know he is the one who performs what the Father has taught him *(the Good work; the first Works)*; doing nothing of himself, alone *(but rather; functioning within the will of God)*. He said; "He that sent me is with me; He has not left me alone

— because I always do those things that please Him.' And many more people believed on Jesus because of these Words. *(The verses above leave little doubt but that the leaders of Israel did have full understanding of Jesus' deity and authority by the time he was crucified. However; God had already [long ago] condemned Judaism to remain blind [a 'first amendment, only'-religion] until the end-times.)* — **(John 8:12-30)**

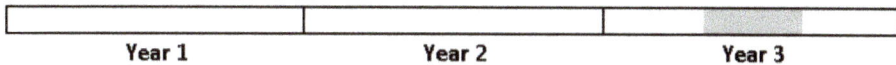

Year 1	Year 2	Year 3

And as Jesus taught at the Temple in Jerusalem, he said (to every man that could believe on him); "If you continue on — hearing and accepting my Word — you will be my disciples. And you will come into possession of the truth *(Holy Spirit of Truth)*. And the truth *(Holy Spirit of Truth)* will make you free *(from the darkness of this world)*." And the Jews said to him; "What are you saying? We are descendants of Abraham; we were never in bondage to any man." But Jesus explained to them that whoever commits sin is the servant of sin. And a servant does not inherit the master's house — but rather; the master's Son does. Jesus said; "If the Son *(Goodness & Truth, the Son)* makes the servant a 'free man' *(paying his sin-debt and saving him)*, then the man is free *(from darkness)*, indeed *(because he now has access to truth/light)*." Jesus told them; "I know you are the 'bloodline' of Abraham — but you seek to kill me because my Word is foreign to you *(because you are blind to it)*. I speak what I have learned from my Father *(Goodness & Truth, the Father)* — and you do what you have learned from your father *(Evil & Error, the Devil)*." They answered Jesus; "Abraham is our Father." But Jesus pointed out to them; "If you were children of faithful Abraham *(children of faith)*, you would be doing the works of Abraham *(the first works; the Good work)* rather than trying to kill me — a man who has told you truth, which I learned from God. Abraham did not do this. Therefore, you do the deeds of your Father." They said; "We were not born of fornication; our Father is God!" But Jesus told them; "If God *(Goodness & Truth, the Father)* were your Father, you would love me; because I *(Goodness & Truth, the Son)* came from God. Think about why you can't comprehend the Words *(truth)* that I speak to you — it is because you cannot hear them." *(These, could not hear the Word [truth] of God because [in truth] they did not 'want' to believe them; because they preferred to do the lustful deeds of their Father, the Devil. These, willingly chose life apart from Jesus — and are, therefore, not ransomed/redeemed [by his blood] from the condemnation of the flesh. They, then, belong to the Devil by default.)* Jesus told them that their Father *(Evil/Error)* was the cause of man's death, from the beginning — because he *(the Devil)* cast down the truth *(in the Garden of Eden)*. Jesus said to them; "When your Father speaks a lie, it originated at him; he is a liar, and the Father of lies." He said that as for them; it is because he tells the truth that they can't believe him — just like their Father *(because they don't want truth)*. Whereas, Children of God are those who 'want' to believe and embrace God's will; therefore, are they able to understand God's Words. — *(John 8:31-47)*

Then the Jews told Jesus; "We have well said that you are a Samaritan *(a half-breed Jew)* and that you have a Devil." But Jesus answered; "I do not have a Devil. I simply honor my Father. And you are trying to dishonor me, but I don't seek my own glory. The one who does seek glory will be your judge. Here is truth: If a man clings to my Words *(Old and New Testament scripture; the first and last amendments)*, he shall never see death." But the Jews replied; "Abraham and all the prophets are dead. Are you saying that you are greater than Abraham and the prophets (who are dead)? Who do you pretend to be?!" And Jesus answered them; "The One you call your God, is the One who honors me; I don't honor myself. I know Him, and proclaim His Words *(as every Christian is called, to do).* Your Father Abraham saw my day and rejoiced in it." But the Jews said; "You are not yet fifty-years-old — how could Abraham have ever seen you?!" And Jesus told them; "I have existed since before Abraham." *(It was, in fact, Christ-the-Son who spoke all of the Old Testament Word to mankind, in addition to the New Testament Word. He is the mouth of God, speaking God's voice.)* Then the Jews picked up stones to throw at him, but Jesus hid himself and slipped through the crowd, escaping. — *(John 8:48-59)*

And as Jesus and the disciples departed from the Temple in Jerusalem, they came upon a man blind from birth. And his disciples asked him; "Master; was it this man's mother, or his Father, who sinned — that this curse fell upon their child?" But Jesus answered; "His blindness was not purposed by God as punishment for anyone's sin — but rather; it was purposed so that the *(Good)* works of God might now be made manifest *(through him)*. I must continue performing the healing works *(the Good works; the first works)* of God for as long as I walk the earth. As long as my light is active *(being manifested)* in the world, I am the light of the world." *(This is a passage that should comfort all suffering Christians; assuring us that we are not always being punished by God, when we suffer. And when we suffer at the Devil's hand, God will always turn it into some eventual benefit to us [or others, in our lives].)* Jesus told his disciples that soon enough, darkness would prevail upon the earth, again *(speaking of the end-times)* — a time when no man of light can work. With that, Jesus spit on the ground to make a clay to anoint the eyes of the blind man. And he told the man; "Go and wash in the Pool of Siloam." And when the man did as Jesus commanded, he came away seeing. Now, when this man's neighbors asked him who had healed him, he told them it was Jesus. And they asked him; "Where is he?" But the man didn't know where Jesus went. — *(John 9:1-12)*

Then, his neighbors brought the healed man to the Pharisees of Israel. And it happened to be on the weekly Sabbath day that Jesus had performed this healing. So (once again), the Pharisees proclaimed that Jesus was not a man of God (because he healed on the Sabbath day). But others questioned how he could not be a man of God — performing such miracles of goodness. So, they asked the healed man; "What do you say, of him?" And the man called Jesus a 'prophet'. So, the Pharisees — eager to prove him wrong — called the man's parents forward. But his parents confirmed only the transformation *(healing)* of their son, and directed their attention back to their son *(fearing the Jews; because the Jews had already published that anyone confessing Jesus to be Christ would be put out of the Synagogue)*. So the Pharisees told the healed man; "Give God the praise, since we know that Jesus himself is a sinner." And as they argued the miracles of Jesus among themselves, the healed man spoke out to the Pharisees, saying; "Never in our history is their record of a man healing another man's blindness —

until now. If Jesus were not of God, he could not perform such healings." At that, the Pharisees accused the healed man of being a sinner from birth *(being born blind)* — and they cast him out of the Synagogue.

- *(John 9:13-34)*

Now, when Jesus heard that the Pharisees of Israel had cast the man out of the Synagogue *(for worshipping him)*, Jesus went and found the man, and asked him; "Do you believe on the Son of God?" And the man said; "Who is he, Lord, that I might believe on him?" And Jesus answered; "You have seen him work — and it is he to whom you are speaking, now." And the man said; "Lord, I believe." Then Jesus told the man; "I came into the world to judge who *(of the blind)* should be given sight, and who *(unwilling to see)* should be made blind." And some of the Pharisees heard what Jesus said, and asked him; "Are we blind, also?" Jesus told them that if Israel were blind *(had no knowledge of God or Jesus)*, they would have no sin. But Israel professes to see and speak the truth of God *(all the while, rejecting Jesus, because they do not want to acknowledge/honor the truth of his testimony)*

— so, they are guilty of sin. *(They are guilty of taking the name of God, in vain.)* **- (John 9:35-41)**

So, Jesus said; "Here is truth: anyone who tries to enter the sheepfold *(to guide the sheep; the lovers of Goodness & Truth)* by sneaking in some other way than entering through the door provided *(which is Christ Jesus; seed of Holy Spirit of Truth)*, that man is a thief and a robber. But the 'true' shepherd *(possessing the seed of the Holy Spirit of Truth)* will enter through the door provided *(through the seed of the Holy Spirit of Truth)* — because the attendant will open the door, to him. And when the 'true' shepherd *(Christ Jesus; seed of Holy Spirit of Truth)* calls his sheep *(the gentle and faithful; lovers of Goodness & Truth)* by name, they follow him; because they know his voice *(Goodness/Truth)*. They will not follow a stranger *(Evil/Error)*, but will flee from that one (not recognizing the stranger's voice)." Jesus said; "I am the door of the sheep. Everyone who ever tried to get to the sheep before me *(not possessing the seed of Holy Spirit of Truth)*, were thieves and robbers. But my sheep *(the gentle and faithful; lovers of Goodness & Truth)* did not hear them." Jesus told them;

"I am the door of the sheep; if a man enters the sheepfold by me *(as a part of the Body of the True Shepherd; Goodness & Truth)* he shall be saved, and shall go in and out and find pasture *(feeding, and being fed)*. The thief *(Evil/Error)* comes to steal and kill, but I have come to give them life, and more abundantly. I am the Good Shepherd." And Jesus explained to them; "The Good shepherd gives his life for the sheep *(living a self-sacrificing life)*. But the hired-hand (whose own, the sheep are not); when he sees the wolf coming *(the devourer)* — he runs and leaves the sheep. Then the wolf catches the sheep and scatters them." He told them; "I lay down my life for the sheep *(of Israel)*. And other sheep I have, also — which are not of the people of Israel; them, also *(the Gentiles who eat the crumbs that fall from the children's table)*, I must bring. They, too, hear my voice *(Holy Spirit of Truth)* and follow me. And there shall be one fold and one shepherd." Jesus told them; "This is why the Father loves me: Because I lay down my life so that I may reclaim it again. No man takes my life from me; I lay it down of my own will. I have the power to lay it down and to reclaim it — and I received this commandment from my Father." And again Jesus' Words caused a division among the Jews; some, saying; "He has a Devil". Others, saying; "Can a Devil open the eyes of the blind?" - *(John 10:1-21)*

After these things, the Lord appointed seventy others from among his disciples, sending them out in pairs of two into every city. *(Now, the Bible doesn't say that Jesus called these seventy men 'apostles' [as he had the first twelve he sent out] — and, yet; that is exactly what they were. A 'disciple' is a pupil who accepts the doctrine his master teaches. But an 'apostle' is a disciple who [afterward] goes forth teaching that same doctrine.)* And Jesus told these seventy apostles; "The harvest is truly great, but the laborers are few. Pray the Lord of the harvest to send laborers into his harvest *(shepherds and bishops of souls)*." And he sent them out as lambs among wolves — with the same instructions he had given to the Twelve Apostles when he sent them; heal the sick and preach that the Kingdom of God has come *(in other words — 'Go perform the first works; replenish the earth with Goodness & Truth')*. And he told them to take no extra provisions with them. Jesus said; "Hail no one along the thoroughfares *(where people are scurrying after the cares of the world)*. And whenever you are about to enter into someone's house, say — 'Peace *(Goodness & Truth)* be to this house'. If the Son of Peace be there *(Christ, the Son)*, your peace will rest upon it *(you will be welcomed)*. But if not; it will return to you *(the occupants will throw your greeting back in your face)*. Lodge in that house — eating and drinking whatever they give you — for the laborer is worthy of his meal *(so it's ok to eat what they provide)*; and do not go from house to house." *(The above verses are very telling. The serving Christian is not instructed to go out into the world all alone — but rather; we are to go out in pairs of two. There is a very good reason for that. We will need to look into a mirror, from time to time in our walk, to find encouragement and the reminder of who we are and who's strength backs us in the battle — as well as needing some degree of protection from complete vulnerability [there is strength in numbers]. We are also not instructed to set up our base-camp in the devil's lair [in the lap of evil]; we are instructed to secure a safe, strong Christian base-camp from which to operate.)* And whatever city you enter; if they are willing to receive you as my disciples, it's OK to eat whatever they set before you *(it is 'clean' [as long as you thank God for it and bless it])*. Jesus goes on, to say; "But if a city refuses to receive you, kick the dust of that city off of you, and say — 'Even the dust of your city, which sticks to us, we wipe off against you. But know that the Kingdom of God has come to you'." And he said; "He that hears you, hears me *(the voice of Goodness & Truth)*. And he that despises you despises me. And he that despises me despises Him *(Goodness & Truth, the Father)* that sent me." **— (Luke 10:1-16)**

And so, the seventy new apostles went out into the country as Jesus bid them. Later, they returned again to Jesus (full of joy), saying; "Lord, even the devils are subject unto us through your name." And Jesus told them; "I saw Satan fall from heaven as a bolt of lightning. I give you power to tread on *(spiritual)* serpents and scorpions and all powers of evil, and nothing shall hurt you. And yet, I tell you; rejoice because your names are written in heaven — not, because the spirits are subject to you." And

Jesus rejoiced in that hour; thanking God for hiding His power from the wise and prudent and revealing it, instead, to the hearts of spiritual infants. Jesus said; "All things are delivered to me of my Father, and only I know Him. But so will every man to whom I *(Goodness & Truth, the Son)* will reveal Him." And he turned to his disciples, and said; "Blessed are the eyes that will see what you are seeing *(the 'manifestations' of the Son of God)*. Many prophets and Kings have longed to see and hear them — but have not." — *(Luke 10:17-24)*

Just then, a certain Lawyer of Israel stood up and asked Jesus; "Master, what is required for me to inherit eternal life?" Jesus answered; "What does the Law of Moses say?" And the man answered; "That you must love the Lord your God with all your heart, soul, strength and mind — and love your neighbor as yourself." Jesus said; "That's right. If you do that, you will have eternal life." But the man pressed Jesus further — asking; "And who is my 'neighbor'?" And so, Jesus told him a parable about a man who was attacked by robbers while on a journey. He had been stripped and wounded, and left for dead on the side of the road. And when a priest of Israel came upon the injured man lying on the side of the road; instead of helping the injured man, he walked around him and continued on his way. And then another Levite of Israel came upon the man and he, too, passed him by. Finally, a Samaritan man came upon the injured man — and he picked him up and carried him safely to an Inn, where he anointed his wounds with salve and gave the Inn keeper money to nurse the man back to health; promising to make up any difference in cost, upon his return. Then, Jesus asked the Lawyer; "Which of these men do you think was a 'neighbor' to the injured man *(willing to help a soul in need)*?" And the Lawyer said; "The one who showed mercy to the injured man." And Jesus told him; "Go now — and do the same." *(Was it the loveless priest who Jesus identified as a Christian's 'neighbor' [or, 'kindred spirit']? Was it the unconcerned, uninvolved Levite? Was it the injured man? No; Jesus clearly establishes that he is referring to 'the man with a sacrificial heart' as our 'neighbor'[in the Kingdom of God]. This is the man we are to love 'as ourselves'; our fellow-laborer in the effort to heal broken mankind.)* — **(Luke 10:25-37)**

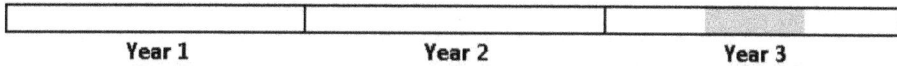

And it came to pass — as they walked and preached — that they entered into the city of Bethany where Martha received Jesus into her house *(which was also the house of Mary and Lazarus, and may have been the same home as that of Simon the Leper)*. And her sister's name was Mary *(the Magdalene)* — who loved to sit a Jesus feet and listen to his Word. But Martha took offense at this; asking Jesus to tell Mary to get up and help her prepare and serve the guests. Jesus told her; "Martha, you are concerned about many things. But Mary has chosen that one 'good' thing which is most needful *(worshipping Jesus)*; and it shall not be taken away from her." — *(Luke 10:38-42)*

And again it came to pass — as Jesus was praying in a certain place — that when he stopped praying, one of his disciples asked him; "Lord, teach us how to pray correctly — as John taught his disciples." And Jesus said; "When you pray, pray like this — 'Our Father, who is in heaven, Hallowed be your name. Your kingdom, come. Your will be done on earth as it is in heaven. Give us, today, our daily bread *(the Word;*

which we need to ingest each/every day). And forgive us our sins, as we forgive those who sin against us. And lead us not into temptation, but deliver us from evil — for, yours is the kingdom and the power and the glory, forever." Jesus told his disciples that God will never refuse to provide them with anything they need *(to tend His flock)*; that they have only to ask for it. He explained that whereas a man may not always be willing to get out of bed (in the middle of the night) just because there is a 'friend' knocking at his door — he certainly would get up if the friend's 'situation' were urgent enough (for the sake of the urgent matter). Jesus said, therefore; "Ask, and it will be given to you. Knock and it shall be opened to you. He that seeks *(inquires)* will find." He told them that their heavenly Father will give the Holy Spirit of Truth to those children who ask Him for it. *(God has made so many blessings available to his children. But He has one requirement; we can't receive them until we first ask for them.)* **— (Luke 11:1-13 (also see; Matt 6:9-15)**

And again when Jesus had cast out a Devil (so that a mute man could speak), he was accused of casting out devils by Beelzebub. But Jesus said, again; "Every kingdom divided against itself will fall. If Satan be divided against himself, how would his kingdom prevail? And if I could only possibly be casting out devils by Beelzebub, by whom do your children *(Jewish priests)* cast them out? Therefore, your children will be your judges. But if I, with the finger of God, am casting out devils — no doubt the kingdom of God is come upon you." *(Then Jesus went even further; to explain the dire importance of inviting and receiving him into your heart [as your new master] after those unclean spirits have been evicted from your soul. There is grave danger in leaving that space vacant.)* Jesus told them that whenever someone stronger than the master of the house arrives *(in your soul)*, he overcomes the master of the house and takes away all his armor that he trusted in. *(As the master of our fleshen 'house', Jesus cannot be overtaken by the devil - but whenever the only master of our soul is our own [weak] will, our soul remains easy prey for the powers of darkness.)* Jesus told them that anyone who is not with him *(serving God, with Jesus)* remains against Jesus *(and, remains vulnerable to unclean spirits)*; that, anyone who isn't gathering with Jesus is scattering *(by default)*. Jesus explained to them, in depth; "When an unclean spirit is driven out of a man, it wanders around looking for a new home *(a new soul to inhabit)*. If it can't find a new home, it will try to return to the man it was cast out of. If it finds that man's body swept clean *(prepared for a new master [by repentance and water-baptism])* — yet, *still without a new master (because he failed to invite Jesus inside, to become his new master)*, then; the unclean spirit enters back into that man (taking along seven other spirits more wicked than itself) — and the last state of that man is worse than the first." — *(Luke 11:14-26)*

And Jesus said; "Blessed are they that hear the Word of God and keep it *(believing it; loving it)*. This is an evil generation that seeks a sign *(for 'proof'; because of the rebellion of their hearts)* — but only the sign of Jonah (and the whale) will it get. The Ninevites repented when they finally heard Jonah *(a 'channel' for the voice of Christ)* preach my Words *(after Jonah finally stopped rebelling against God's will for him to preach to Nineveh)* — and someone greater than Jonah is preaching to you, now." He said; "A man doesn't light a candle to hide it in a secret place; he lights it so that he can light up the whole house." *(The above verse is Jesus telling us, in no uncertain terms, that we are not supposed to seek our own salvation so that we can go hide safely in a corner until the rapture; we have been saved/enlightened for the purpose pouring that Goodness & Truth out into the world so that others may be drawn to Christ through our efforts. When we refuse to let the Holy Spirit live through us in this way, God sees us as a 'dead' branch and cuts us off.)* Then Jesus explained to them that when a man sees things through the light of a single eye *(meaning; through the heavenly mind of Christ)*, his whole body is filled with light *(Goodness & Truth)*. But when a man sees things through the dim light of an evil eye *(meaning; through a corrupted, worldly mind)*, his whole body is filled with darkness *(Error/Evil)*. And Jesus pointed out that it's each man's job to choose which light will fill him. – *(Luke 11:27-36)*

And again Jesus was invited by a Pharisee of Israel to dine with him. And Jesus went in, and sat

down to eat. And, this Pharisee *(like all the others,*
before him) marveled that Jesus did not wash his hands
before he ate. So, Jesus said to him; "You Pharisees
clean the outside of yourselves — but your inside is
full of ravening and wickedness. You fools; didn't the
same God who made the outside, make the inside, too?"
And Jesus told them, plainly, that if they would
simply give back to God that which God had entrusted
to them *(goodness, love, right judgment, etc...),* they
would be clean on the outside and on the inside.
Instead; they tithe herbs (to God) *(things of worldly*
value), while they neglect better *(spiritual)* things
like righteous judgment and the merciful love of God.
(God needs and expects men to pour into the world the
same grace that he pours onto them. This is the only
way that mankind can be saved.) And Jesus (again)
condemned the Lawyers and Pharisees — because they
covet the most prestigious seats in the Synagogues,
and greetings in markets. He called these self-seekers
'graves' that men aren't aware of. Then, a Lawyer
stood up and said; "Master, you are reproaching us,
also." And Jesus said; "Yes — you too. You weight men
down with heavy burdens that not even you would

attempt. You prove that you allow the deeds of your Fathers: for they indeed killed the prophets, and you build their tombs. Therefore, this generation *(those who blaspheme the Holy Spirit of Truth)* will be held accountable for every prophet ever killed — beginning at righteous Abel. You Lawyers of Israel have taken away the 'key' of knowledge *(the wisdom of Christ)*. Not only did you refuse to enter in through the gate *(Christ Jesus)*, but you also prohibit other people from entering." Thereafter, the Pharisees and Lawyers of Israel tried desperately to provoke Jesus into saying something they could use against him. — *(Luke 11:37-54)*

In the meantime; the crowds were growing so thick that the people were stepping on top of each other. And Jesus began teaching them, saying; "Beware of the leaven of the Pharisees of Israel (which is hypocrisy). Their (hypocritical) deeds will be brought to light. And do not be afraid of those who can only kill the body. Fear Him who has the power to kill the body and cast you into hell for eternity." But again he told them; "Take heart; not even a sparrow is forgotten before God — and you are far more valuable to God than a sparrow." Jesus said; "Whoever will confess *(faith in)* me to other men — him, will the Son of man confess to the angels of God. And you shall be forgiven; even if you have spoken a word against the Son of man *(the soul of Jesus)*. But if you blaspheme against the Holy Ghost *(Holy Spirit of Truth)* *(as the Serpent did)*; that, will never be forgiven. And when you are brought into the Synagogues — before magistrates and powers (being persecuted) — don't worry about what to say; the Holy Ghost *(the Holy Spirit of Truth)* will speak through you, in those moments." — *(Luke 12:1-12)*

And Jesus told the multitudes; "Beware of covetousness — because a man's life doesn't consist in things *(of worldly value)* that he owns." He went on to tell them a parable about a rich man whose harvest was so bountiful that he didn't have enough room to store it all — so, the man decided to tear down his barns and build bigger ones. Afterward (he thought), he could rest easy for many years. But God called the man a fool for laying up *(physical)* treasure for himself rather than *(spiritual treasure)* toward God. And God took his life, that very night. *(The moment this man 'agreed' with the temptation, he was already 'guilty' of the sin; because that was the point at which he embraced and planted the seed of the sin.)* Therefore, Jesus told his disciples they should take no thought for their physical life; he promised them that God will provide for them. He asked them; "How much better are you, than the fowl of the air — which God feeds?" He told them that if they would seek the Kingdom of God, first *(serving God, in the pursuit of healing and saving souls),* God would provide them with everything they would ever truly need. Jesus told them; "Sell everything you have and give to the poor. Provide yourselves bags that won't fall apart and a treasure in heaven that will never fail — where no thief can break in and steal it." He told them; "Wherever your treasure is *(that which you value)*, that's where your heart *(your desire)* will be, also." — **(Luke 12:13-34)**

Jesus told the Lost Sheep of Israel *(the gentle and faithful; the Good & True)*; "Arm yourselves with my Word, and *(with your lights burning)* wait upon the Lord to return from the wedding *(at the Second Coming)*; so that when he comes and knocks, you may open to him without hesitation. Blessed are those servants who he shall find ready *(loving and serving Christ)* when he arrives. And if the goodman of the house had known what hour the thief would come, he would have watched — and his house wouldn't have been broken up." *(In other words; we can't prepare against dangers that we can't [or, won't] acknowledge.)* Jesus went on, to say; "Be ready; for the Son of man will return when you do not expect him." And Peter said; "Lord, do you say this to us alone *(Christianized Jews)* — or, do you say it to everyone?" And Jesus told him that when the Lord returns; the servant he finds feeding the sheep *(tending the flock)* is the servant he will make ruler over everything he has. But when he finds a professed 'servant' of God living according to his own will instead of God's will; the Lord will take that servant by surprise and judge him as an unbeliever — and that man will be punished more than the man who erred as a result of having no knowledge of God, at all *(because he will have been given all the knowledge he needed, to serve God productively)*. Jesus explained that to whomsoever much *(enlightenment and power)* is given — of him, much is expected. —

(Luke 12:35-48)

Jesus said to them; "I came to send the Holy Ghost into the earth. But I have a rebirth to be baptized with *(his willing death, and resurrection)*. And I did not come to give peace upon the earth, but rather division. Family members will be set against one another, because of me." Jesus marveled at how his people *(prepared-Israel)* can so easily discern and predict acts of nature — but somehow, cannot discern the time that is at hand *(or, judge what is right from wrong, among themselves)*. He told them that when a man is going before a judge with his adversary, he should try very hard to work things out with him, along the way (lest the judge cast him into prison, as proposed) — because once a man is imprisoned, he will pay all. Then he told them a parable about a farmer who had a particular fruit tree in his vineyard which hadn't produced fruit in three years. Because it would not produce fruit, the farmer told the husbandman to cut down the useless tree. But the husbandman begged the farmer on the tree's behalf; asking to be allowed just one year to fertilize it and give special attention to it — after which time, if the tree should begin to produce fruit again, it might be saved. *(This is how*

*Jesus has intervened to save mankind [which, was
already condemned].) — (Luke 12:49--13:9)*

And it came to pass that Jesus was again teaching
in the Synagogue on the weekly Sabbath day — and
there, he saw a woman hunched over before him. So,
Jesus laid his hands on her and said to her; "Woman,
you are loosed from your infirmity." And the woman was
immediately made straight, and glorified God.
Therefore, the ruler of the Synagogue became indignant
and spoke out against Jesus for healing her on the
Sabbath day. But Jesus — calling the ruler an
hypocrite — once again pointed out that it is always
good to do 'good' on the Sabbath day. He said to the
onlookers; "Don't each of you loose your ox on the
Sabbath day and lead him away to water? So, then,
shouldn't this daughter of Abraham be loosed from
Satan (who has had her bound these eighteen years) on
the Sabbath day?" And with these Words, Jesus shamed
all of his adversaries — and the people rejoiced in
his miracles. *(It is the works of the world that we
are commanded to refrain from, on the Holy day; not,
the first works.)* Then Jesus told the people; "The
Kingdom of God is like a grain of mustard seed, when

it is planted and grows into a great tree that
shelters all the fowls of the air. And the Kingdom of
God is like the leaven that a woman hides in a little
flour — which grows to permeate the whole batch of
bread dough." — *(Luke 13:10-21)*

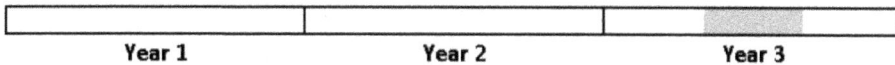

Year 1	Year 2	Year 3

And they were in Jerusalem, at the Feast of the
Dedication — and it was winter. And Jesus walked in
the Temple in Solomon's Porch. And the Jews came and
surrounded Jesus, saying; "Tell us plainly; are you
the Christ, or aren't you?" But Jesus answered them;
"I told you, and you didn't believe me. The works that
I do in my Father's name bear witness of me. But you
do not believe — because you are not of my sheep *(the
gentle and faithful; the Good & True)*. As I have said;
my sheep hear my voice *(Truth/Goodness)* and follow me
— and I give them eternal life. And no man shall pluck
them out of my Father's hand. I *(Goodness & Truth, the
Son)* and my Father *(Goodness & Truth, the Father)* are
one *(Goodness/Truth)*." With that; the Jews picked up
stones to stone him. But Jesus asked them; "For which
of the good works that I've done, will you stone me?"

They answered; "Not for a 'good' work, but for blasphemy; saying you are equal to God." But Jesus pointed out that it is written in the scripture where the Word of the Lord said; "Ye are Gods" *(speaking of those, whom the Lord has 'sanctified' and sent into the world, in His name — and the scripture cannot be broken.)* And Jesus asked the Jews; if the Lord himself called those who receive His Word 'Gods' — why, then, were the Jews calling Jesus a blasphemer for saying he is 'one with God'? He told them; "If I don't do the works of my Father, then don't believe me. But if I do; then believe the works even if you don't believe this 'man' standing before you — so that you may know, and believe, that the Father and I are one." But once again, they sought to take him by force. So, Jesus escaped and went away again beyond Jordan; to the place where John first baptized (Bethany & Bethabara) — and there, Jesus abode *(no doubt, in the home of Mary and Martha and Lazarus).* And many came to him, there; saying that although John didn't do miracles — everything he had said about Jesus was true. And many believed on Jesus, there. —
(John 10:22-42)

So, Jesus went about teaching in the neighboring cities and villages, again; working his way back around to Jerusalem. And along the way, someone asked him; "Lord, are there only a few who will be saved?" And Jesus told them that any man entering the kingdom at the strait gate *(through Jesus Christ)* would be saved. *(Not so long ago, Jesus had explained that he is the 'gate' to the sheepfold — and that only a true Shepherd would be able to pass through that gate to tend the sheep.)* Now, Jesus would tell them that a great many souls will 'want' to enter in to the sheepfold, but will not be able to. *(These, will no doubt be those souls who seek the safety of the fold, but are never willing to 'serve' [as a Shepherd].)* Jesus explained that once the master of the house rises and shuts his door, anyone who decides to knock afterward will not be permitted inside. Then; those locked out will plead; "Lord, we ate and drank with you — and you taught us your Word." But the master will tell them; "Depart from me, you who worked iniquity *(rather than the work of God; the first works)*; I never knew you." *(Souls are healed and saved in order to go forth healing and saving [allowing the*

*Holy Spirit to live 'through' us]. This is how Christ
'knows' us; when he has lived 'through' us.)* Jesus
told them that there will be weeping and desperation
when those *(unproductive)* men see the 'fruit'-
producing servants in the Kingdom of God, while they
themselves are locked out. Jesus said; "And behold;
there are last which shall be first. And *(a remnant of
the)* first which shall be last." *(Jesus refers to
Israel as 'the first' [they are the children of the
'first' covenant] — and, he refers to Christians as
'the last' (they are the children of the 'last'
covenant. In the end-times, the Christian Church will
be harvested from the earth, first [these are the
souls who possess and proclaim both of the Two
Witnesses/Amendments from God; the Old Testament Word
and New Testament Word]. These, will be harvested at
the end of the 3.5-year 'Sorrows-Period' [half way
through the 7-year 'Sorrows & Tribulations Period'].
Afterward; a fractional Remnant of Israel [144,000]
will be harvested [at the end of the 3.5-year
'Tribulations-Period'].)* **– (Luke 13:22-30)**

The same day, there came certain of the Pharisees
of Israel, telling Jesus; "Get out of here before

Herod *(the Jewish Tetrarch)* kills you!" But Jesus told them that a prophet must remain in Jerusalem; therefore, he must do the work of God among them today and tomorrow — and be perfected on the third day. Then Jesus said, aloud; "Oh Jerusalem, how often would I have gathered your children together as a hen gathers her chicks under her wings — but you refused." Nevertheless; he told them that Judaism *(the 'one amendment, only' religion)* will remain 'blind' until the end times — because they refused him. — *(Luke 13:31-35)*

And it came to pass that Jesus went into the house of one of the chief Pharisees of Israel to eat bread on the weekly Sabbath day. And they watched him. And there, Jesus saw a man who suffered from the dropsy. So Jesus asked, aloud; "Is it lawful to heal on the Sabbath day?" But no one answered him. Therefore, Jesus healed the man. Then Jesus asked, aloud; "Which of you would not rescue an ox or an ass on the Sabbath day, if it fell into a pit?" And again, no one would answer him. So, Jesus *(perceiving that this crowd was willing to hear his teaching)* began to teach all those who were present. He taught them that whenever they are bidden to a wedding, they should always sit in the least important seats, humbling themselves *(lest someone more important show up, and the host demand their seats from them; humiliating them)*. Better, they should assume the humble position and the host might ask them to switch to a more important seat. This, he taught them, because in the Kingdom of God; whoever exalts himself will be humbled, and whoever humbles himself will be exalted.

- (John 14:1-11)

Then Jesus began to teach the Pharisee who was hosting the dinner. He told him that whenever he invites guests over for a meal, he shouldn't invite those who could easily return the favor *(robbing himself of a blessing from heaven)*. Better, he should invite the poor, the maimed, the lame and the blind *(those who couldn't possibly repay the kindness)*, because then he would be blessed and recompensed at the resurrection of the just *(giving, to those in need)*. And someone who sat with him spoke out, saying; "Blessed is he that shall eat bread in the Kingdom of God." This inspired Jesus to tell them a parable — a story about a host who prepared a great feast and invited many choice companions of his city. But when his servant went to collect the guests at suppertime, all of the guests had something else they would rather be doing — so, they all asked to be excused from the invitation. The master became angry and told the servant to go out and collect from the midst of the city all the poor, the maimed, the lame and the blind *(souls who would appreciate a nourishing meal)*. And when the servant had collected them all, there were still many empty seats to fill. So, the master told the servant to go out into the thoroughfares and hedges beyond the city, and gather anyone else who was hungry — so that his house would be filled *(because the master was determined that none of those original guests [who refused to fellowship with him] would taste of his supper)*. — **(Luke 14:12-24)**

Then Jesus turned his attention to the multitudes that had followed him, there. He told them plainly that if anyone thinks to become his 'disciple' — having not yet chosen Christ *(the Holy Spirit of Truth)* above family and friends and substance (and even over his own life) — that man cannot be a disciple of Christ. He also told them that whoever is not willing to carry the burden of God's work — as a servant — cannot be a disciple of Christ. *(Jesus reasoned with them, that any man planning a construction project [or, planning a battle] has to 'know' how many tools (or, weapons) are available to him [and, dependable] — because, he cannot begin the project [or, the war] until he knows he has enough resources to get the job done.)* Jesus said; "Salt is good. But if the salt has lost its savor, what will season the salt? It's no good for any purpose, then." *(Again; we have been healed and saved in order to go forward healing and saving — enlightened; in order to go forth sharing that enlightenment. What good are we to God, if we refuse to pass on the same grace that we have been blessed with?)* **— (Luke 14:25-35)**

And as the tax collectors and sinners drew nearer to Jesus, the Pharisees and Lawyers of Israel murmured about it. So Jesus put a parable before them. He asked; which man among them — if he had 100 sheep, and one became lost — would not go out and find the lost one; searching, until he found it? Afterward, rejoicing in its recovery? He told them that this is how the angels in heaven rejoice over every single sinner that is brought to repentance. Then, he told them another parable; this one, about a man who had two sons. The youngest son received his inheritance early, and left home with it. Immediately seduced by everything the world had to offer, he wasted his entire inheritance tending to the assorted weaknesses of his own flesh. Afterward, he was left to fend for himself (slopping another man's pigs, and having to eat what they ate). Eventually, the young man was humbled to the point where he welcomed the idea of returning home — even if only to serve his own father. He reasoned that in his father's house, even the servants were always well fed. When he arrived at his father's home, the repentant young son would say to his father; "Father, I have sinned against heaven and against you, and I am no more worthy to be called your son. Please have me, as your servant." But Jesus told them that the loving father of such a repentant son (ever watching for that son's return) would see him coming from a great way off, and would run to his son (falling on his neck and kissing him) — and that he would immediately reinstate him as his son; being once lost, and now found. — *(Luke 15:1-24)*

But then Jesus continued the story; describing how offended the older son became when the younger son was welcomed back home with a party: Upon hearing the celebration inside the house, the older son was overcome with jealousy and anger, and he refused to enter into the house. Therefore, the father came outside to persuade him. The older son was angry that he had loyally worked for his father, always — and yet, his Father had never celebrated his presence so lavishly. But his father told him; "Son, you are with me always and everything I have is yours. Your lost brother's return warrants celebration; he was 'dead' — but, is now alive again." - *(Luke 15:25-32)*

Then Jesus told them a new parable; about a wicked steward who had irresponsibly wasted his master's assets when he was expected to put them to good use. After his miscarriage of responsibility, the steward learned that he was going to lose his authority (and his home), due to his neglect — so, he began to consider what he could possibly do, to be welcomed into the houses of others; so, that he wouldn't be left homeless. Arriving at a plan, he began to call everyone else who owed the rich lord money; and he warned each man to pay the rich lord at least a portion of whatever they owed. And the rich lord commended the unjust steward for discerning a wise course of action; for offering himself as a productive servant to his lord (if only, by leading other debtors to be productive toward their lord). *(He had produced the fruit of 'good judgment', which was acceptable to his Lord.)* Jesus told his disciples, that; the Gentiles of this world have wisely (and faithfully) concluded that it doesn't pay to focus on their own will — but rather; on God's: They have determined to serve God by producing fruit for Him *(whereas, Judaism had stopped producing fruit to Him).* Jesus impressed upon his disciples that the children of light *(the Lost Sheep of Israel)* should not disregard the 'value' God had sewn into these Christians — because God will one day use these Christians to receive them into heaven. *(In the end-time, it is the horrific events of the harvest of the Christian Church [the 'Two Witnesses'] that God uses to open the eyes of the 144,000/Remnant of Israel - so that they can finally believe in Jesus, and be saved.)* Jesus taught them that any man who can be trusted to leave the world behind and perform the harder work of gathering unrighteous strays and rebels into God's flock — surely that man has the best interest of the flock at heart *(rather than his own comfort)*. His work *(sacrificially healing and saving souls)* is proof that he is not serving two masters at once. And the Pharisees of Israel *(who were covetous of their own earthly position)* heard these Words and tried to discredit Jesus. But Jesus told them; "You Pharisees justify yourselves before men — but God knows your hearts. What men esteem highly is abomination in God's sight." He explained that, first; the *(Old Testament)* Laws and Prophets provided mankind the 'example' of what heavenly order looks like — and now (at last), the Kingdom of God is preached *(the New Testament Word; which, actually restores that heavenly order)*. He told them that every man must embrace this last amendment *(the Word of Jesus Christ)*; Jew and Gentile, alike. Jesus said that it is easier for heaven and earth to pass away than for any part of the Law to fail; that all men and women who are separated from God, exist in an 'adulterous' state *(a condition, for which, God provided a cure, through Jesus). — (Luke 16:1-18)*

Then Jesus told them another parable; about a certain rich man and a poor sick beggar *(whom Jesus called 'Lazarus')*. In this story, the rich man fared sumptuously every day, while the poor, sick beggar lay miserably at his gate every day *(begging for the crumbs that fell from his table)*. And when the poor sick beggar finally died, the angels carried him into Abraham's bosom. But when that rich man died, he was delivered into hell. Looking up from the torments of fiery hell, the rich man could see the poor man resting in Abraham's bosom — and he cried out to Abraham to send the poor man to quench his horrible thirst. But Abraham said to him; "Don't you remember how in life you lacked for nothing, while this poor man lacked for everything? Now is the time of his comfort and your torment. And besides; there is this impassable gulf between us, which none of us can traverse." So, the rich man began to beg Abraham to at least send the poor man to warn his family to repent. But Abraham told him that the living already have Moses' Laws and the testimony of the Prophets *(in other words; the Old Testament Word)* to guide them. And if they refuse to hear *(and accept)* Moses and the Prophets *(rebelling against the Word of God)*, not even the 'resurrection of the dead' *(the New Testament Word)* could persuade them. *(This parable is not an account of an actual event that took place [as many people understand it to be]. Jesus used parables to present a concise and accurate snapshot of a truth that he was trying to convey [affording us the same benefit that 'experience' yields over 'book-learning']. This parable is Jesus' way of saying; "If people in the grave could talk — this is the discussion they would have." In this parable, the 'rich' man is meant to represent the leaders of Israel [who were richly blessed by the Word of God; responsible for raising a nation in the nurture and admonition of Goodness & Truth — but dropped the ball]. And the 'sickly beggar' is meant to represent all the world's souls who were left begging for scraps of God's truths, because of it. Jesus was telling the story of how the leaders of Israel mishandled God's Word — and how Goodness & Truth overcame their*

corruption by continuing to focus on willing faith.) —
(Luke 16:19-31)

Then Jesus told his disciples; "Offenses must
come — but woe to the man through whom the offenses
come." Then, Jesus taught his disciples how to spare
the Kingdom of God such losses, going forward;
chiefly, through forgiveness *(each Christian soul
having the power to cover a multitude of sins)*. He
taught them they should rebuke a brother *(fellow-
Christian)* who offends them — and if that brother
repents, they must forgive him. In fact; as many times
as their brother *(a fellow Christian)* is willing to
repent and ask forgiveness, they are to forgive him.
The disciples said to Jesus; "Increase our faith."
Jesus told them; "If you have faith as small as a
mustard seed, you can command a tree to pick up and
move itself, and it will obey you." He went on to
explain that the children of God wrangle and tend and
feed the 'strays' of God's flock — for the purpose of
presenting them to God 'whole', someday. Obeying God's
direction to do this is the whole duty of a servant of
God. *(Each Christian soul has the power to keep
offending souls out of hell, by forgiving them.*

Likewise, each Christian soul has the power to refuse to forgive the sins of others [and those sins will remain unforgiven on earth and in Heaven (Matt 16:19)]. But if we slay our bucking brothers [by refusing to forgive them] we would not be serving God's purpose. Jesus was saying that offensive behavior is the whole reason our work is necessary — therefore, it's going to be around until the job is finished.) — (Luke 17:1-10)

And it came to pass, that as Jesus passed through Samaria and Galilee, he entered into a certain village and was hailed by ten lepers. They called out to Jesus; "Master, have mercy on us." So, Jesus told them; "Go and show yourselves to the priests of Israel." And as they obeyed — walking along their way to the priests — they were all healed. But only one of them (a Samaritan) returned, to give glory to God — thanking Jesus. Jesus told him; "Go your way. Your faith has made you whole." *(Always — in every instance of healing or answered prayer — 'faith' must be present. Faith is the lump of clay from which God forms each miracle.)* And the Pharisees of Israel demanded that Jesus tell them when the Kingdom of God would come. But Jesus explained to them that it's not as though they will see the kingdom coming — but rather; the kingdom will rise up inside of men. — *(Luke 17:11-21)*

And Jesus told his disciples that the day is coming when they will desire to see one of the days of the Son of man — but they won't be able to see one *(in the end-time)*. And at that time, the world will say, 'over here'...or, 'over there'. But Jesus said; "Do not believe them." He said that just as lightning flashes in one corner of the heavens and shines clear to the other side; that's how the return of the Son of man will be *(at the Second Coming; when Jesus returns for the 144,000/Remnant of Israel)*. And in that day, the whole world will be carrying on like they do every other day; oblivious of what is about to come. And just as it was when Lot removed himself from Sodom, and its destruction followed immediately, so it will be in the day the Son of man returns *(as soon as the children of Goodness & Truth are harvested from the earth, whore-mankind will be utterly destroyed)*. Jesus told them; "In that day; if someone is on their rooftop, but his belongings are in the house; do not try to run into the house to gather anything. And if someone is out working in the field, he should likewise not try run back to his house for anything (because Lot's wife was destroyed when she looked back)." He said that whoever shall seek to save his earthly life in that day, will lose it. And whoever is willing to part with his earthly life in that day, will (thereby) preserve his eternal life. He said that in that day; where two women are grinding together, one will be taken and one will be left behind. And where two men are working in the field; one will be taken and one will be left behind. And his disciples asked him; "Where will this happen, Lord?" And Jesus told them that wherever the Body (of Christ) may be; there, will the eagles be gathered together *(the angels of God)*. Nevertheless, before all this; Jesus, himself, must suffer many things and be rejected by his own. — *(Luke 17:22-37)*

And Jesus told them another parable; teaching them that men ought always to pray, and not to grow weary of it. This was a story of a king who feared God but had no regard for men — and a widow who lived in his city that came to him with a complaint. Jesus said

the king ignored the woman's complaints for as long as
he could, but when the woman refused to stop badgering
him for help, he finally dealt with her problem (just
so that she would stop hounding him about it). Jesus
told his disciples; "Hear the message the unjust judge
is sending *(in other words; 'Alright...just stop
badgering me!')*. And shall not God avenge His own
children (which cry to him day and night) — even
though He may leave them crying, for a long time? I
tell you that He will — and soon." Then Jesus asked;
"Nevertheless; when the Son of man returns, will he
find this kind of faith on the earth?" — *(Luke 18:1-8)*

Then Jesus told a parable for the benefit of
anyone who trusts in their own righteousness (while
judging other people as 'sinners'). He told them a
story of two men who went into the Temple to pray; one
was a Pharisee of Israel, and the other was a tax
collector. The Pharisee prayed; "Thank you God, that I
am not a sinner like that tax collector over there."
But the tax collector — standing far away — wouldn't
even look upward (for his shame). And he prayed; "God;
be merciful to me, a wretched sinner." And Jesus told
his audience that the tax collector — not, the

Pharisee — would go home justified; because, everyone who exalts himself will be abased, and he that humbles himself will be exalted. — *(Luke 18:9-14)*

And when Jesus finished speaking, he departed from Galilee and came into the coasts of Judea, beyond Jordan — still in route to Jerusalem. And a great multitude followed him, and he healed many people. The Pharisees of Israel also came to him; tempting him. They asked Jesus; "Is it lawful to Divorce your wife." Jesus asked them; "What does the Law of Moses say, about divorce?" They said; "Moses allowed a writing of divorcement to put away one's wife." Then, Jesus explained to them that it was only because of the hardness of their hearts that Moses ever wrote that particular law. Jesus said that when God made man, He made him in two halves; male and female. And, that for this cause *(for the two to become one)* a man shall leave his Father and mother and cleave to his wife — the two, becoming one flesh. And what God has joined together, let no man put asunder. Later, Jesus' disciples would ask him again of the matter, and Jesus would tell them that a person who gets a divorce for any reason other than fornication *(intercourse, outside of marriage)* — and marries someone else — is guilty of adultery. Also; that whoever marries the person divorced for committing fornication (or, the guiltless person who has been unjustly divorced) is also guilty of adultery. That said; God does not require that every man must be married; only, that when a man is married, he should honor its Holy estate. — *(Matt 19:1-12 & Mark 10:1-12)*

And when some in the crowd began to bring little children to Jesus to touch and to pray over; Jesus' disciples rebuked them. But Jesus was very displeased with this. He told them to let the little children come to him, because the Kingdom of Heaven is made up of exactly such innocent, humble beings as these (*obedient to authority and trusting everything*). He told them; "Whosoever shall not receive the Kingdom of God the way a little child does, shall never enter therein." And he took up the children, in his arms, and blessed them. And then he departed from there. — *(Matt 19:13-15 & Mark 10:13-16 & Luke 18:15-17)*

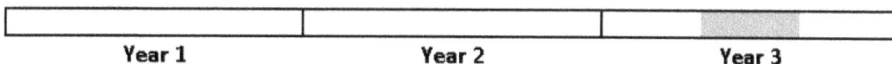

Year 1	**Year 2**	**Year 3**

And when Jesus was gone forth into the way, a certain rich young ruler came running and kneeled before him; asking; "Good master, what good thing shall I do, that I may have eternal life?" And Jesus said; "Why do you call me 'good' — only God is good." And he told the young man that to have eternal life he must keep the commandments of God. The rich young ruler answered; "I have kept all of these, from my youth, up." - *(Yet clearly, there was something in this young man's heart whispering that God wanted more from him). (Now, the Bible doesn't say whether Jesus was already acquainted with this young man, or, if Jesus simply knew him 'from afar off' [as he had 'known' Nathanael before actually meeting him (John 1:47-49)] — but this passage states that Jesus loved this rich young ruler.)* Therefore, Jesus told him; "There is one thing you still lack if you wish to be perfect; go and sell everything you have, and give it to the poor. Thereby, you will have treasure in heaven. And take up the cross *(die, to the world)* and follow me." *(Being 'perfect' is only the end-result of the process of growing in one's Christian anointing. This young man was already safely on the path to* *perfection [as many of us are], but he had asked specifically what he needed to be 'perfect' [immortal image of God], and Jesus answered him honestly; 'give up everything earthly — including, your own physical life'.)* And when the young man heard that he must sell everything he had (to be 'perfect'), he went away very sorrowful *(for he was very rich).* (This passage doesn't say that the rich young ruler 'refused' to trade his wealth for a place in heaven; it only says that he was very sad to learn that he must. In fact; some people believe this rich young ruler was Lazarus [whose wealth was already being applied to the ministry of Jesus indirectly; through his sisters, Mary (the Magdalene) & Martha]. How overwhelming such a prerequisite would have seemed to a young man who may have just come into sudden wealth at an unusually young age. Lazarus did, in fact, eventually give all [see; John 11:5, 36 & 12:2]. In life, Jesus had said that his own Father loved him because he always does 'those things which please' God. Perhaps, foreknowing this young man's eventual complete sacrifice would explain why Jesus was said, in this passage, to have* *loved him so much.) — (Matt 19:16-22 & Mark 10:17-22 & Luke 18:18-23)*

And Jesus told his disciples; "Here is truth: a rich man shall hardly enter into the Kingdom of Heaven; it is easier for a camel to go through the eye of a needle than for a rich man to enter into the Kingdom of God *(having too much baggage)*." And when his disciples heard this, they were astonished; wondering how, then, anyone could be saved *(how could anyone survive if they had no resources to meet their needs?)*. But Jesus told them these things (which aren't possible with men) are possible with God; because all things are possible with God. And Peter said to him; "Lord, we have left all, to follow thee." And Jesus told him; "Here is truth: you who follow me, will sit upon twelve thrones, judging the twelve tribes of Israel in the Kingdom of Heaven. And everyone who has forsaken houses...or, brethren...or, sisters...or, father...or, mother...or, wife...or, children...or, lands for my name's sake; they shall receive an hundredfold now, in this lifetime (along with persecutions), and inherit everlasting life. But many that are first *(the children of the first covenant; Judaism)* shall be last *(harvested)* — and the last *(children of the last covenant; Christianity)* shall be first *(harvested)."* — *(Matt 19:23-30 & Mark 10:23-31 & Luke 18:24-30)*

Jesus explained that the Kingdom of Heaven is like a man who owned a household; who, went out early one morning to hire laborers into his vineyard. And he agreed to pay them one penny per day — and he sent them to work early in the morning. A few hours later, he saw other men standing idle in the marketplace, and so he hired them also; agreeing to pay them whatever is right at the end of the day. And again, later, he did the same. And still later; again. Finally, at evening he sent his steward to call in all the laborers, to pay them (beginning with the last hirelings, first). And he paid them all one penny for the day's work. But, the laborers who had been working all day long felt they should receive more pay than the laborers who had only worked a couple hours (at the end of the day). But, the householder said; "Friends — I haven't done you wrong; you agreed to do the work for one penny — take it and be content. What I give to these others is mine to give. Is your eye evil, because I am good?" And so, the last shall be first and the first last; for many are called, but few are chosen. - *(Matt 20:1-16)*

And as Jesus was going up to Jerusalem, he took the Twelve Apostles aside — and he told them that when they get to Jerusalem, the Son of man will be betrayed to the Chief Priests and Lawyers of Israel — and they will condemn him to death. He told them that these *(Jewish)* men would deliver him to the Gentiles to mock, and to scourge, and to crucify him — but he would rise from the grave three days later. Jesus' disciples could still not understand any of it *(because they did not want it to be true)*. - *(Matt 20:17-19 & Mark 10:32-34 & Luke 18:31-34)*

Then came forward James and John (the sons of Zebedee) with their mother — asking Jesus to promise that James and John may sit by his side in the kingdom when Jesus comes into his glory. They asked him to place one of them at his right hand, and the other, at his left. But Jesus said to them; "You do not understand what you are asking. Are you able to drink from the cup that I shall drink of — and to be baptized with the baptism that I am baptized with?"

And they answered; "We are able." And Jesus told them that (in fact) they will. However, Jesus told them that to sit on his right hand, or his left, was not his to give — but rather; that it will be given to them for whom it was prepared, by God. And when the other ten disciples heard their request, they were indignant against James and John for thinking they were more important than the rest *(according to this passage, John and James were not terribly humble men)*. So, Jesus explained again that the princes of the Gentiles exercise great authority over the Gentiles — but it shall not be that way among Christians. Rather; the one who is greatest among Christians will be the one who ministers to them and serves them *(just like the example Jesus was setting for them; having come here to minister to others and give up his own life, to save them)*. — *(Matt 20:20-28 & Mark 10:35-45)*

And being near Jericho, a great multitude followed Jesus. And blind Bartimaeus (the son of Timaeus) sat begging by the side of the highway. And when he heard that it was Jesus of Nazareth who passed by, he began to cry out; "Son of David, have mercy on me." And the multitudes rebuked him — that he should be quiet. But, he cried out all the more — until Jesus finally stopped and called him forward, asking the man; "What do you wish me to do to you?" And the man said; "Lord, that I might receive my sight." And Jesus told him; "Go your way — your faith has made you whole." And immediately, he received his sight and began to follow Jesus, glorifying God. And all the people who saw it gave praise to God. — *(Matt 20:29-34 & Mark 10:46-52 & Luke 18:35-43)*

And Jesus entered and passed through Jericho, surrounded by the multitudes. And there came a rich man named Zacchaeus (the chief tax collector) seeking to get a glimpse of him — but he was unable to see Jesus through the throngs of people, because he was very short. So, he ran ahead of Jesus and climbed up into a sycamore tree, to look. And when Jesus passed by that tree, he looked up and saw Zacchaeus — and he said to him; "Zacchaeus, come down from the tree, for today I must abide at your house." And Zacchaeus made haste to come down, and he received Jesus joyfully. And then the crowds began to murmur against Jesus — saying that he went to be the guest of a 'sinner'. But Zacchaeus told Jesus; "Behold, Lord; I will give half of my goods back to the poor. And whatever I have taken by false accusation, I will restore it fourfold." And Jesus told him; "Today is salvation come to this house; for you, also, are a son of Abraham *(an obedient son of faith)*, and the Son of man came to seek and to save that which was lost *(the faithful and obedient)*." — *(Luke 19:1-10)*

And since everyone's attention was drawn to his conversation, Jesus threw in a parable *(because he was near Jerusalem, and all the people still expected the Kingdom of God to suddenly 'appear' one day; all at once)*. He told them a story of a certain nobleman who went into a far country to receive the title to his kingdom *(to return again to his kingdom, afterward)*. So, the nobleman called his servants and gave them money, saying; "Handle my business until I return." But the citizens of his land hated him — and they sent a message after him, saying; "We will not have this man to reign over us." And it came to pass, that when he returned *(having received the title to his kingdom)* he called to him the servants with whom he had left his wealth — to find out how much each man had gained by trading in his business. One servant came, saying;

"Lord, your pound has gained ten pounds." And the king said; "Well done good servant; since you have been faithful with a little, you may have authority over ten cities." And the second servant came, saying; "Lord, your pound has gained five pounds." The king said, likewise, to him; "Well done. You may have authority over five cities." — *(Luke 19:11-19)*

But, when the third servant came, he said; "Lord, here is your pound; I have kept it safe in a napkin — for I feared you, because you are an acentric man, taking up what you have not laid down, and reaping what you did not sow." And the king said to him; "I will judge you out of your own mouth, you wicked servant. You knew that I expected my wealth to be increased. Why, then, did you not at least put my money into a bank where it could earn interest?" With that, the king ordered the money to be taken from his hand and given to the servant who had doubled his money. He said; "Unto everyone who has *(increase)*, more will be given. And from him that has not *(increase)*, even the little that he has shall be taken away from him. And my enemies who said they would not suffer me to reign over them — bring them here, and slay them before me." *(Again; when we are redeemed into the Kingdom of God, it is for the purpose of increasing the Kingdom of God — not, so that we can sit safely in a corner selfishly clinging to our own salvation.)* Then did Jesus turn him about and continue on his way, toward Jerusalem — and the multitudes followed him. **— *(Luke 19:20-28)***

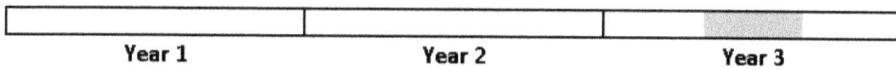

Year 1	**Year 2**	**Year 3**

Now, a certain young man was sick, named Lazarus — who, was from Bethany; the hometown of Mary *(the Magdalene)* and her sister Martha *(and Simon the Leper)*. This was the same Mary which anointed the Lord with ointment and wiped his feet with her hair — whose brother, Lazarus, was sick. Now, Jesus loved Mary and Martha and Lazarus *(a fact specifically mentioned, in this passage and several others)*. Therefore, when Lazarus fell ill, his sisters sent to Jesus, saying; "Lord, he whom you love is sick." And when Jesus heard that Lazarus was sick, he told his disciples that his sickness was not unto death — but rather; for the glory of God; so that the Son of man might be glorified, through the occurrence. Therefore, Jesus

remained right where he was, for two more days.
Afterward, he told his disciples; "Let us go into
Judea again." But, his disciples said; "Master, the
Jews have tried to stone you recently — and you want
to go back into Judea?" And Jesus answered them; "Are
there not twelve hours in a day? If a man walks in the
day, he doesn't stumble *(because he walks by the light
of God)*. But, if a man walks at night, he stumbles
(because there is no light in him)." That said, Jesus
told them; "Our friend Lazarus sleeps. But I go to him
so that I may awake him out of sleep." The disciples
answered; "Lord, if Lazarus is sick, isn't he better
off asleep?" Then, Jesus told them plainly that
Lazarus was dead — adding; "And I am glad for your
sakes that I was not there to stop his death; to the
end that you may believe. Nevertheless, let's go to
him, now." *(Perhaps it was Jesus' love for Lazarus
that had inspired him to apply the name 'Lazarus' to
the poor sick beggar in his earlier parable [who made
it into Abraham's bosom, when the rich man couldn't].
In fact; it may have been that very parable, that very
day, which gave the real Lazarus his first inkling
that God was calling him to apply his wealth to Jesus'*

*ministry. In any event; by this time in Jesus'
ministry, Lazarus had indeed become a treasured friend
and ally to Jesus and the disciples — because Thomas
would now say to the others; "Let us all go to
Lazarus, that we may die with him.")* — *(John 11:1-16)*

Later, as Jesus and the disciples drew near to
Bethany, they learned that Lazarus had lain in the
grave for four days, already. Now, Bethany was near
Jerusalem *(almost two miles away)*. And many of the
Jews came from Jerusalem to comfort Martha and Mary
concerning their brother's death. *(I believe this is
yet another indication of the wealth of this family.)*
And as soon as Martha heard that Jesus was near, she
went to him — saying; "Lord, if you had been here, my
brother would not have died. But I know that even now,
whatever you ask of God, He will give it to you." And
Jesus told her that her brother would rise, again. To
that, Martha replied; "I know that he will rise again
in the resurrection, at the last day." But Jesus told
her; "I am the resurrection — and the life. He that
believes in me; though he were dead, yet he will live.
Whoever lives and believes in me shall never die. Do
you believe this, Martha?" And she answered; "Yes,

Lord. I believe that you are the Christ, the Son of God which was promised to come into the world." That said; she went and called her sister Mary, secretly, saying; "The Master is come, and he calls for you." And as soon as Mary heard it, she arose quickly and came to where Jesus was — in a place just outside of town. And the Jews which were with her in the house followed Mary *(thinking, at first, that she arose to go to the graveside of Lazarus; to weep)*. — *(John 11:17-31)*

And as Jesus neared the village where they had buried the deceased Lazarus, Mary ran to Jesus and threw herself down at his feet, saying; "Lord, if you had been here, he would not have died." When Jesus saw Mary weeping — and the Jews also weeping with her — he groaned in the spirit and was troubled *(their sorrow was breaking his heart)*. He asked them; "Where have you laid him?" And they said; "Lord, come and see." Then Jesus began to cry, himself — and the Jews said; "Behold how Jesus loved Lazarus!" And some said; "Couldn't this man, who opened the eyes of the blind, have kept this man *(whom he loved)* from dying?" And as they drew near to Lazarus' grave, Jesus again groaned in himself *(heartbroken, for their sorrow)*. Now, there was a large stone that lay across the opening of the cave where Lazarus was laid. And Jesus said, to some; "Take away the stone." But, Martha said; "Lord, by this time, he stinks; for he has been dead four days, now." And Jesus said; "Did I not tell you that if you would believe, you would see the glory of God?" So, they took away the stone. And Jesus lifted up his eyes, and said; "Father, I thank you that you have heard me. And I knew that you hear me always — but, for the sake of these people which stand near, I said it out loud; so they may believe you have sent me." And when he had finished speaking, he cried with a loud voice; "Lazarus; come forth." And Lazarus *(who had been dead four days)* arose and came forth — bound hand and foot with grave-clothes. And his face was bound about with a napkin. Then, Jesus told them; "Loose him, and let him go." — *(John 11:32-44)*

From that moment; many of the Jews which had come to Mary in her hour of need *(and saw the things which Jesus did)*, believed on Jesus. But, some went straightway to the Pharisees of Israel, and told them all that Jesus had done. Then the Chief Priests and

the Pharisees gathered together a council, and said;
"What do we do? This man does many miracles. If we
leave him alone, all men will believe on him." But at
that moment, Caiaphas (who, was the High Priest, that
year) spoke out — saying; "You *(fellow Jews)* know
nothing — nor, do you consider that it is beneficial
for Israel that one man should die to save the people,
and that the whole nation not perish." Now, Caiaphas
(being a Priest of God) didn't say these words of
himself; it was the Holy Spirit prophesying through
the High Priest; rehearsing how Jesus should die for
Israel *(whereas; it had been prophesied long ago that*
Christ would not only die to save Israel — but also,
that his death would gather together the children of
God who were scattered abroad.) Nevertheless; the
Chief Priests and Pharisees received the words of the
High Priest, gladly — because they wanted Jesus dead.
Therefore; Jesus could no longer walk openly in Jewry
after raising Lazarus from the grave — so, he went
into a country near the wilderness of ungodly man;
into a city called Ephraim, to await his final hour. —

(John 11:45-54)

CHAPTER 4 — PRE-CRUCIFIXION WEEK

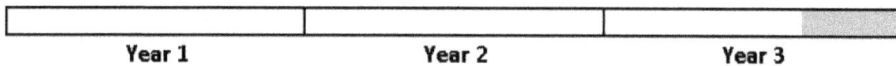

Year 1	**Year 2**	**Year 3**	

*(FIVE DAYS before CRUCIFIXION) beginning at 6:00 p.m.:

And when the Annual Feast of the Passover drew near *(at the end of Jesus' third year of ministry)*, many Jews went up to Jerusalem (prior the start of Passover) to purify themselves. And as they stood in the Temple, they wondered among themselves whether Jesus would come to the feast, or not — because, the Chief Priests and Pharisees of Israel had given a commandment that if any man knew where Jesus was (at any time) they must report it to the council. Now, it was the sixth day before Passover Day (just five days before Jesus would be crucified). And Jesus entered again into Bethany, where Lazarus was (whom Jesus had raised from the dead). And they made Jesus a supper, in Bethany; at the home of Simon the Leper — *(See; Fig. 1, below)*.

(Fig. 1 -- PRE- Crucifixion Week):
(On the Hebrew Calendar, each new 'day' begins at 6:00 p.m. [not, midnight]):

		FRI	SAT	SUN	MON	TUE	WED	THU
(Night time)		6:00 PM: (Return to Bethany) (Mary anoints)	6:00 PM: (Return to Bethany)	6:00 PM: (Return to Bethany)	6:00 PM: (Return to Bethany) (End-time Prophecies Foretold) (Jesus tells Parables)	6:00 PM: (Return to Bethany) (Greeks arrive)	6:00 PM: (Jesus eats Last Supper) 10:00 PM: (Garden) 12:00 AM: (Interrog'n) 5:00 AM: (to Pilate)	6:00 PM: (Jewish Passover) (First 'night' in the grave)
		5:59 AM	5:59 AM	5:59 AM	5:59 AM	5:59 AM	5:59 AM	5:59 AM
(Daylight)		6:00 AM: (Entrance into Jerusalem)	6:00 AM: (Fig Tree cursed) (Tables turned, in Temple)	6:00 AM: (Fig Tree withered) (Authority Challg'd) (Jesus tells Parables)	6:00 AM: (Mary anoints) (Judas betrays)	6:00 AM: (Prep for Last Supper)	6:00 AM: (Interrog'n & Torture Ends) 9:00 AM: (CRUCIFIED) 3:00 PM (DIED) 5:00 PM (BURIED)	6:00 AM (First 'day' in the grave)
		5:59 PM	5:59 PM	5:59 PM	5:59 PM	5:59 PM		5:59 PM
							Preparation Day	Feast of the Passover

(This is the first time that 'Simon the Leper' is actually referred to, in the Gospels. Again; he may have been the Father of Mary and Martha and Lazarus, and may also have been 'Simon the Pharisee', mentioned

in Luke 7:36-40.) And Martha served the meal, but the risen Lazarus *(whom Jesus loved)* sat at the table with Jesus and the rest of his disciples *(and would no doubt continue to sit at the table with them, throughout this entire last week of Jesus' life)*.

(As we follow along with the table, above; bear in mind that on the Hebrew calendar [beginning at Gen 1:4-5], a 'day' consisted of twelve hours of darkness [first], followed by twelve hours of daylight. This is opposite of what modern man considers a 'day', and it makes the Gospel timeline very complicated to follow, if we're not careful.)

And Mary took out a pound of ointment of spikenard *(which, was very expensive)* and anointed the feet of Jesus, and wiped his feet with her hair — *(See; Fig. 1 [pg. 178])*. *(This was the second time Mary had anointed Jesus' feet.)* Then, spoke out Judas Iscariot (who, would later betray Jesus), and said; "Why wasn't this ointment sold — and the money, given to the poor?" Now, Judas didn't ask because he cared for the poor — he asked, because he was a thief and he carried the money purse for the group. And Jesus said to him; "Leave her alone. She has anointed me for the day of my burial. The poor, you will always have with you, but you won't always have me, with you." And many Jews knew that Jesus was there, and came to him; not just to see Jesus, but also, to see Lazarus (whom he had raised from the dead). Therefore, when word of Jesus' whereabouts reached the Chief Priests of Israel, they also began to consider how they might put Lazarus to death; since many of the Jews were come to believe in Jesus, because of him. — *(John 11:55—12:11)*

On the following morning (of that same day; daytime following evening), Jesus passed by Bethphage on the way into Jerusalem — *(See; Fig. 1 [pg. 178])*. And Jesus sent two of his disciples out into the village to find a donkey and a colt (the foal of a donkey), to bring them back to him. This, they did — and when they returned with them, they laid their clothes upon the donkeys and sat Jesus upon the foal *(When I picture this scene in my mind, I imagine that God was symbolically riding the adult donkey; as a symbol of being by Jesus' side). (And these events had come to pass just as they were foretold by prophecy; in Zechariah 9:9.)* And a very great multitude spread their garments in the path before Jesus, as he continued on to Jerusalem. Still others cut down branches of palm trees and strewed them in the way, before him. And all the while, the crowds called out to Jesus; "Hosanna to the Son of David; blessed be the king that comes in the name of the Lord. Hosanna in the highest." And some of the Pharisees of Israel (who were among the crowd) said to Jesus; "Master, rebuke your disciples *(for, they had called him their 'king')*!" But Jesus told them that even if he could quiet down the people, the stones would immediately cry out the same thing. And the Pharisees said; "You see how we avail nothing; the whole world is going after him." And when Jesus was come near to Jerusalem, he looked upon the city — and Jesus began to cry, again. He said to Jerusalem; "If you had known — at least in this, your day — all the things which belong to your peace. But now are they hid from your eyes; for the days will come upon you that your enemies will cast a trench about you, and surround you — and you shall be leveled to the ground (and your children with you). Not one stone will be left upon another — because you did not recognize the time of your visitation." And when Jesus finally entered into

Jerusalem *(on this; the sixth day before the Feast of the Passover)* all the city was moved, saying; "Who is this?" And the multitudes answered them; "This is Jesus; the prophet of Nazareth of Galilee." And Jesus entered into the Temple on that first day *(as if drinking in the last moment of calm, before the storm)*; and, having looked around at all things (and evening was now approaching), he went out of Jerusalem again; returning to Bethany with the Twelve — *(See; Fig. 1 [pg. 178])*. — **(Matt 21:1-11 & Mark 11:1-11 & Luke 19:29-44 & John 12:12-19)**

*(FOUR DAYS before CRUCIFIXION) beginning at 6:00 p.m.:

There, in Bethany (at the home of Simon the Leper), Jesus ate dinner with his disciples and retired for the evening. When morning arrived *(of that same day; daytime following evening)*, Jesus and his disciples would return to Jerusalem. As they walked from Bethany to Jerusalem, Jesus saw a fig tree off in the distance — and whereas the tree was covered with leaves, Jesus approached it in search of fruit. But, when he came to the tree, it was fruitless (because, it was not yet the time of year for fruit-bearing).

And, Jesus used the occasion for a lesson; he said to the tree (in front of his disciples); "Let no man eat fruit from you, ever again." And they walked away from the tree, leaving it cursed — *(See; Fig. 1 [pg. 178])*. When they entered into Jerusalem *(that second day)*, Jesus went directly into the Temple of God. And finding the Temple full of merchants, he began to cast out all those who bought and sold, there; overthrowing their tables and chairs — *(See; Fig. 1 [pg. 178])*. And he would not suffer any man to carry a vessel through the Temple. And as he cast them out, Jesus asked them; "Is it not written, 'My house shall be called the house of prayer'? But, you have turned it into a den of thieves." And the blind and the lame came to Jesus in the Temple, and he healed them. And as the Chief Priests and Lawyers of Israel watched him — and heard the children calling out to him, 'Hosanna to the Son of David' — they were very displeased. They told Jesus; "Do you hear what these people are saying?" And Jesus answered; "Yes. And have you never read, 'out of the mouths of babes and sucklings you have perfected praise'?" And the Chief Priests and Lawyers wanted desperately to destroy Jesus — but they were afraid of him, because all the people were astonished at his doctrine. Then, Jesus left them and went out of the city again, to lodge in Bethany — *(See; Fig. 1 [pg. 178])*. *(In the personal accounts of Matthew and Luke regarding Jesus' return to Jerusalem at the start of pre-crucifixion week, they each first mention Jesus' arrival in the city, and then proceed directly into their account of Jesus cleansing the Temple [failing to make mention that a sunset and a sunrise occurred between those two events, as noted in Mark 11:12]. If both of these events had occurred in the same day — as it appears, in his report — this would actually eliminate one full day that Jesus spent in Jerusalem that week as reflected by the rest of the Gospel timeline.)* — **(Matt 21:12-19 & Mark 11:12-19 & Luke 19:45-48)**

*(THREE DAYS before CRUCIFIXION; beginning at 6:00 p.m.):

There, in Bethany (at the home of Simon the Leper), Jesus ate dinner with his disciples and retired for the evening. When morning arrived *(of that same day; daytime following evening)*, they walked again from Bethany to Jerusalem. When they passed by the fig tree that Jesus had cursed the previous day, they found the tree was shriveled from the roots, up — *(See; Fig. 1 [pg. 178])*. Peter called it to remembrance, saying; "Master, the fig tree which you cursed is withered away already!" And Jesus taught them, saying; "Have faith in God. If you have faith, and do not doubt, you can tell this mountain to remove itself and it will be done. Whatsoever things you ask for in prayer, believe that you will receive them and you will receive them. And when you stand *(before God)* asking for something, forgive *(if you have anything against anyone)* — so, that your Father in heaven may forgive your sins. Because, if you are unwilling to forgive others, your Father in heaven will neither forgive you of your sins." — ***(Matt 21:20-22 & Mark 11:20-26)***

And having entered, again, into the Temple in Jerusalem, the Chief Priests and the Elders of Israel came directly to Jesus as he was teaching, and said; "By what authority do you these things? And who gave you this authority — *(See; Fig. 1 [pg. 178])*? "And Jesus answered their question with a question of his own. He said; "I will ask you a question. And if you answer me, I will answer you in the same way: the baptism of John; was it of heaven, or, of men?" And they struggled to find a way to answer Jesus' question — because, they knew that if they said John's baptism was 'from heaven' Jesus would ask them, 'Why, then, did you not believe John's testimony?'. But, if they said John's baptism was 'from men', they feared the people would riot *(because, the people held John as a prophet of God)*. So, they finally answered; "We cannot tell *(which translates: 'It wouldn't be convenient for us to answer your question')*." And Jesus told them; "Neither do I tell you the answer you seek *(which translates: 'It wouldn't be convenient for me to answer yours, either')*." **— (Matt 21:23-27 & Mark 11:27-33 & Luke 20:1-8)**

Then Jesus asked them a question of judgment. He said; "Tell me what you think: A certain man had two sons — both, of whom, he asked to go and work in the family's fields. The first son answered *(rebelliously)*: 'No, sir!' — but later, he repented of his selfish attitude and went and worked in the fields. The Second son had answered *(obediently)*; 'Yes, sir — I go now.' — but for one reason or

another, he never made it out into the fields." Then,
Jesus asked; "Which of his two sons did the will of
his Father?" They answered; "The first son." And Jesus
told them they were right — adding; "Here is truth:
the tax collectors and harlots will enter the Kingdom
of God before you will — because, when John *(the
Baptist)* came to you (telling you how to make things
right), you didn't believe him. But the tax collectors
and harlots did believe him. And when you saw the end
result of their obedient faith *(their transformation
and redemption)* you still did not repent afterward,
that you might believe him." — *(Matt 21:28-32)*

And Jesus said; "Hear another parable..." — *(See;
Fig. 1 [pg. 178])*. And he told them a story of a
certain householder who planted a vineyard, and got it
up and running — and then, let it out to husbandman
while he went into a far country. And when the time of
harvest drew near, he sent his servants to glean his
fruit from the husbandmen who tended his vineyard. But
the husbandmen beat and killed his servants. So, the
Lord gave them another chance; sending other servants
to collect the harvest from the husbandmen. But,
again; they beat and killed those servants. Finally,

the lord sent his own son to collect the harvest —
thinking that surely they would reverence his son. But
when those evil husbandmen saw the heir of the
vineyard coming, they decided that if they just killed
the heir they could keep the vineyard for themselves —
so, they killed his son, also. Then, Jesus asked the
Chief Priests and Elders of Israel; "When the Lord of
that vineyard returns, what do you think he will do to
those wicked husbandmen?" And the Chief Priests and
Elders answered; "He will miserably destroy those
wicked men — and let out his vineyard to other
husbandmen who will render him the fruits in their
seasons." And *(amazed)* Jesus said to them; "Have you
never read the scripture that says, 'The stone which
the builders rejected is become the head of the
corner; this is the Lord's doing, and it is marvelous
in our eyes'?" Jesus said; "This parable is a picture
of the very reason the Kingdom of God will be taken
away from the nation of Israel and given to a nation
willing to bring forth the fruits, thereof. Whosoever
trips over this stumblingblock will be broken — but,
on whomsoever it falls; it will grind him to powder."
- *(Matt 21:33-46 & Mark 12:1-12 & Luke 20:9-19)*

Then Jesus told them another parable — *(See; Fig. 1 [pg. 178])*. He told them the Kingdom of Heaven is like a king who prepared a marriage feast for his son. And when he sent his servants to call the *(intended)* guests, they would not come. So, the king prepared and sent forth other servants *(which, were trained in all the details of the lavish feast that had been prepared for the guests)*. But still, they were not willing to set aside their own plans to share in their king's joy. Worse, yet; some of them beat and killed the servants he had sent to them. And when the king heard of the evil that had been recompensed for his loving invitation, he was very angry. And he sent forth his armies to destroy those murderers and to burn up their city. And whereas those guests had not been worthy; the King sent his servants out into the highways to bring back as many willing guests as they could gather (both of the good, and of the bad). And so, the wedding was furnished with guests. And when the king came in to see the guests, he saw there a man which did not have on a wedding garment *(eluding to his garment of light; his white robe)* — so, the king asked the man; "Friend, how have you entered herein, without a wedding garment?" And the guest was speechless; he didn't understand *(He had allowed his garment of light to become darkened)*. Then the king told his servants to bind the man hand and foot, and cast him into outer darkness. Jesus told them; "There will be weeping and gnashing of teeth; for many are called *(invited)*, but few are chosen *(being faithful servants)*." - *(Matt 22:1-14)*

Thereafter, the Pharisees of Israel conspired with the men of Herod *(the Tetrarch of Israel)* and sent spies to Jesus — that they should try to entangle him in his conversation *(so they could arrest him and deliver him to the Roman Governor, Pontius Pilate)*. And so, they did bait Jesus — saying; "Master, we know that you teach the way of God, in truth, and that you have no respect for the person of men. So, tell us; is it lawful to give tribute to Caesar, or not? *(which is to say; is it lawful to pay taxes, to Caesar?)*". But Jesus perceived their wicked intentions and said to them; "Why do you tempt me, you hypocrites? Show me a piece of the tribute money." And they gave Jesus a Roman penny. So, Jesus studied the penny, and then he asked the spies; "Whose face is this, on the penny?"

They said; "Caesar's." And Jesus said; "Well then;
render to Caesar what belongs Caesar — and render to
God, what belongs to God." - *(Matt 22:15-22 & Mark
12:13-17 & Luke 20:20-26)*

The same day, the Sadducees of Israel came to him
(who, believe there is no resurrection). These, asked
Jesus a question of the afterlife, saying; "Moses said
that if a man dies, having born no children with his
wife, then his brother must marry his wife and raise
up children to his name. But answer this: If a woman
married seven brothers in a row — each of whom, died
without producing any children with her — and lastly,
the woman also died; whose wife would she be, in the
resurrection — since they all had her, to wife?" And
Jesus told them; "You are in great error; not knowing
the scripture — nor, the power of God. In the
resurrection they do not marry, but exist like the
angels of God in heaven *(no male/female distinction)*.
And concerning that the 'dead' are resurrected: Do you
not recall in the scripture where God said, 'I am the
God of Abraham, Isaac and Jacob'? This means that God
is not the God of the dead — but rather; of the
living." And again the multitudes were astonished at

his doctrine. – *(Matt 22:23-33 & Mark 12:18-27 & Luke 20:27-38)*

And when the Pharisees heard that Jesus had put the Sadducees to silence, one of the Lawyers *(judging that Jesus had answered well)* asked Jesus; "Which is the greatest commandment of them all?" And Jesus answered; "It is, to love the Lord your God with all your heart, soul, mind and strength — this is the first commandment. And the second is like it: Love your neighbor as yourself. There is no other commandment greater than these." And the Lawyer said; "You have said the truth; for, there is one God, and no other but He. And to love him with all your heart, understanding, soul and strength — and to love your neighbor as yourself — these, are worth more to God than all burnt offerings and sacrifices." And when Jesus saw that he answered discreetly *(making his faith known to Jesus)*; Jesus said to him; "You are not far from the Kingdom of God." And since the Pharisees of Israel were also gathered together there, Jesus asked them; "What do you think of Christ; whose son is he?" And they said; "The Son of David." But Jesus asked; "How, then, did David call him 'Lord'? —

saying, 'The Lord said unto my Lord, sit on my right hand until I make your enemies into your footstool'? If David called Christ 'Lord', how then is Christ David's Son?" And no man was able to answer him a word. Nor, did any man, from that day forward, ask Jesus any more questions. And the common people enjoyed just listening to Jesus speak. – *(Matt 22:34-46 & Mark 12:28-37 & Luke 20:39-44)*

And in the audience of all the people, Jesus said to his disciples; "Beware of the Lawyers — who love to walk in long robes...and love salutations in the marketplaces...and the best seats in the synagogues...and the uppermost rooms at feasts — they, who devour widows' houses and, for show, make long prayers. These, will receive greater damnation." Then, Jesus looked up and saw the rich men casting their gifts into the treasury. And then he saw a certain poor widow, who threw in two mites. Jesus told his disciples; "Here is truth: this poor widow has cast in more than all they which have cast into the treasury — for, all these rich men have made an offering of their excess, but she has cast in all that she had; her entire living." – *(Mark 12:38-44 & Luke 20:45–21:4)*

And Jesus continued to teach the multitudes and his disciples. He told them that the Lawyers and Pharisees of Israel sit in Moses' seat *(they rule the nation of Israel)* — and, for that reason, the people should obey everything the Lawyers and Pharisees of Israel 'instruct' them to observe and do. But Jesus warned them not to perform the same works they 'see' them doing (because, although the Lawyers and Pharisees pile heavy burdens and traditions on the people, they don't honor those regulations themselves — and the works they do perform are only done to be seen, of men). They gorge themselves in the upper rooms at feasts, and love to be called 'Rabbi, Rabbi' *(an 'official')*. Jesus told them; "As for you; do not ever be called 'Rabbi' — for, Christ is your Master *(same as every other Christian)*. The greatest among you *(Christianized men)* shall be your servant. Whoever will exalt himself shall be abased, but he who will humble himself, will be exalted." — *(Matt 23:1-12)*

Then, Jesus openly rebuked those who were responsible for misleading the lost people of Israel: He said; "Woe to you, Lawyers and Pharisees of Israel — hypocrites! You shut up the Kingdom of Heaven from men *(by refusing the last amendment; the New Testament Word)*; for you refuse to go in, yourselves neither will you allow (to enter) those others who do want to enter. You compass land and sea to convert one soul to Judaism, and when he is made, you make him twice the child of hell that you are. You blind guides say there is nothing wrong with swearing by the Temple — but that anyone who swears by the gold of the Temple, has sinned. Which is greater; the gold, or, the Temple that sanctifies the gold?! And you say that there is nothing wrong with swearing by the altar — but that anyone who swears by the gift that is upon it, is a sinner. Which is greater; the gift, or the altar that sanctifies the gift?! He who swears by the altar swears by all things that are upon it. And whoever swears by the Temple, swears by God (who dwells within it). And whoever swears by heaven, swears by the throne of God, and by Him that sits upon it." *(In other words; the gift [Jesus Christ] is just as Holy — and just as valuable — as the one who gave the gift; God.)* — **(Matt 23:13-22)**

And Jesus said; "Woe to you Lawyers and Pharisees of Israel — hypocrites! You pay tithes of mint and anise and cummin *(things of earthly value)*, but you refuse to bring forth the weightier fruit of good judgment, mercy and faith *(things of spiritual value; the First Works)* — these, you should not have left undone. You are blind guides, who strain at a gnat and swallow a camel *(lacking the Holy Spirit of Truth, for proper discernment)*. You clean the outside of the cup and platter — but within, you are full of extortion and excess. Clean first what is inside the cup and platter — so that the outside may be clean, thereby. You are like whited tombs, which look clean on the outside — but within, are full of dead men's bones and all uncleanness). Likewise; you appear righteous to men — but within, you are full of hypocrisy and iniquity. You build the tombs of the prophets and garnish the tombs of the righteous — and you claim that you would not have participated in the murders of the prophets (if you had lived in the days of your forefathers). But, thereby, are you witnesses of yourselves; ye are the children of them which killed the prophets. How can you escape the damnation of hell? I will send you prophets and wise men and Lawyers; some of them you will kill and crucify, and some of them you will scourge in your Synagogues — and you will persecute them from city to city. And, thereby, will come upon you all the righteous blood shed upon the earth; from the blood of righteous Abel to the blood of Zacharias (whom you slew, between the Temple and the altar). Here is truth: all these things shall come upon this generation *(those who blaspheme the Holy Spirit of Truth)*." Then Jesus spoke again to Jerusalem, saying; "How often would I have gathered your children together as a hen gathers her chicks — but you *(Leaders of Israel/Judaism)* refused me. Now, your house is left to you, desolate — for you shall not see me again until you say, 'Blessed is he *(Jesus Christ)* that comes in the name of the Lord' *(this will happen when the 144,000/Remnant of Israel get their eyes opened, during the 'Sorrows & Tribulations Period')*." Then, Jesus departed from the Temple. — *(Matt 23:23—24:1)*

*(TWO DAYS before CRUCIFIXION; beginning at 6:00 p.m.):

And as they walked away from the Temple that evening, Jesus' disciples began to discuss all the beautiful features of the Temple. But Jesus told them

a day was coming when there would no longer be one
stone of the Temple left upon another. And when they
had returned to Bethany — *(See; Fig. 1 [pg. 178])*,
Jesus' disciples asked him when these 'end-of-time'
prophecies would come to pass — and what would be the
sign of their coming. And Jesus told them; "Do not be
deceived; many will come in my name — saying, 'I am
Christ, and the time draws near'. Do not believe
them." He explained that there would indeed be a
succession of signs — and everyone would be able to
see them, for themselves. He told them they would hear
of wars and commotions — but they shouldn't be
terrified by it, because their end *(the Remnant of
Israel/144,000)* will not be, yet. He said that nation
will rise against nation and kingdom against kingdom,
and great earthquakes will occur in divers places
around the world, and famines and pestilences. These,
he called the 'beginning of sorrows' *(the first 3.5-
years of the 'Sorrows & Tribulations Period')* *(Mark
13:8)*. He said there would also be fearful sights and
events from heaven. However, he said; "Before all
these things come to pass, the world will persecute
you and deliver you up to the Synagogues and into

prisons. And you will be hated by all nations, for my name's sake *('Savior')* — for a testimony against them *(so they can be marked as a part of the Beast)*." He told them that when this happens, his name's sake will be counting on them for a testimony. Therefore, they should settle it in their hearts not to premeditate about what they might say — because, in those moments, the Holy Ghost will speak wisdom 'through' them which their adversaries shall not be able to oppose or resist. — **(Matt 24:1-9 & Mark 13:1-11 & Luke 21:5-15)**

Jesus said that in those days, Christianized mankind will be betrayed by parents, brethren, children, kinfolk and friends — and some of those, would even cause them to be put to death; because so many will be offended. Also, he said that many false prophets will arise and deceive many. And because evil will be so commonplace in those days, the love of many people will turn cold — but he assured them that not one hair of their head would perish *(from eternity)* if their love could manage to endure until the end; that, by possessing the patience of the Holy Spirit, they will not lose their souls. And he told them the Gospel of the Kingdom will be preached in all the world for a

witness to all nations, before the end would come.
*(And there are two witnesses in the earth; the Old
Testament witness/Word and the New Testament
witness/Word. Those who possess and proclaim both, are
called 'the Body of Christ'.)* Jesus told his disciples
that when the world finally sees Jerusalem *(the
Kingdom of God)* surrounded by armies *(which the Bible
calls, 'the abomination of desolation' [Matt 24:15 &
Luke 21:20])* — then, they can be sure its desolation
is near. He told them that when they see Jerusalem
(the Kingdom of God) surrounded, everyone in Judea
should flee into the mountains and everyone in the
surrounding countries should not enter into Judea —
because these will be the 'days of vengeance',
prophesied of. *(If the whole world decided [all at
once] to destroy all children of God — I imagine that
list would include all professed Jews and Christians.
Also; it makes sense to me that the city of Jerusalem
would be a likely first big target.)* Jesus told his
told disciples this will be a time of great distress
in the land, and wrath upon this people; that many
will be killed by the sword and many will be taken
away captive, into all nations. In those days,

Jerusalem *(the Kingdom of God)* will be trodden down by the Gentiles, until the Gentiles' time is fulfilled. — **(Matt 24:10-16 & Mark 13:12-14 & Luke 21:16-24)**

Jesus said that after these things have taken place *(after the Two Witnesses/body of Christ are destroyed, in the first whore-movement against the Kingdom of God)*, there will be signs in the sun, moon and stars — and on earth, there will be distress of nations (with perplexity); the ocean waves roaring. And men's hearts will be failing them, for fear of those things which are taking place on earth and those things which are coming *(the 'Tribulations Period')*. And he told them to pray that their flight would not come during the 'winter' *(the times after the harvest of the Christian Witnesses)*, nor on the Sabbath day (during which times, mankind will experience greater tribulation than has ever been known to man). He told them that the powers of heaven will be shaken — and that no flesh would be able to survive this 'Sorrows & Tribulations' Period unless those days would be shortened. *(Thankfully, God is going to shorten those days for the Christian Witnesses; for the sake of 144,000 Jews who will be 'awakened' to Christ by the events of the Christian-Witness harvest.)* And Jesus assured them that the whole world will see the Son of man coming in a cloud, with power and great glory *(at the Second Coming)*. He said; "When this happens, look up; for your redemption is near." *(Don't look down, or backward. Don't run. Don't be afraid; our eternal life begins when our physical life ends.)* He told them that if they are on a housetop when this whore-movement begins, don't run into the house *(to gather belongings)*. And, if they are in a field working, don't run home *(to gather belongings)* — just flee from Judea, into the mountains. He told them that just as a man sees buds shooting forth on the branches of a tree and 'knows' that summer is near — so, likewise; when they see these signs, they should know that the Kingdom of God is near *(they should recognize the 'season' that God has described, for them)*. He warned them not to become complacent in the way of the world *(being drunken or distracted from the Word of God)* lest they miss the signs of the time; because the end is going to come as a snare to those who aren't watching for it. Therefore, he told them; "Watch and pray, so that you may be counted worthy to escape all these things that are coming to pass; that you may be able to 'stand' (in right standing) before the Son of man." — *(Matt 24:17-24 & Mark 13:15-20 & Luke 21:25-36)*

Jesus took great care to make it clear that when the Son of man returns *(at the Second Coming; for the 144,000/Remnant)*, it will be apparent to the whole world at once *(the way lightening illuminates the whole sky, at once)*. And he expressed again that his return *(at the Second Coming; for the 144,000/Remnant)* would be after the sun and moon and stars are darkened *(after the harvest of the Christian Witnesses)* and, that he would be arriving with his vast army of angels to harvest them from the four winds; from one end of heaven to the other. Jesus told them that no man can know the day or the hour of his return (not even the Son of man) — but just as we can discern the seasons of nature on earth, we are expected to be able to discern the 'season' of his return *(because he has, now, described it to us)*. And whereas heaven and earth will one day pass away; he assured them his Words will never pass away. And except for the elect (who, watch for his return) he will take the world by surprise.

And he asked, aloud; "Who, then, is a faithful and wise servant whom his Lord (when he comes) shall find, watching (aware)?" Again, he told them that the Son of man is like a man taking a far journey, who gave his servants authority and commanded them to perform certain work for him in his absence — and commanded the porter, to watch. And Jesus told his disciples; "What I say to you (Christianized Jews) I say to everyone (Jews and Gentiles, alike); watch." — **(Matt 24:25-51 & Mark 13:21-37)**

And Jesus told them another parable — (See; Fig. 1 [pg. 178]): He told them that the Kingdom of Heaven is like ten virgins who took their oil lamps and went to meet the bridegroom. Five of them, foolishly neglected to bring enough oil in their lamps — while, the other five virgins cautiously brought oil to spare. Jesus said that as the bridegroom took his time preparing to receive them, the ten virgins fell asleep waiting for him. And when it was announced (at midnight) that the bridegroom was coming for them, they arose and trimmed their lamps. And the five foolish virgins (whose oil had run out) asked the five wise virgins if they could borrow some of theirs. But the wise, answered; "I'm sorry, but there is not enough for both you and us. Go and buy some oil from someone who is selling it." *(In other words; 'You must pay the price.')* And as they were gone away to buy more oil, the bridegroom came — and he took with him those who were ready. And he closed the door behind him. Afterward, came the others — saying; "Master, let us come in." But he answered; "Here is truth: I do not know you." *(Christ the Son [seed of the Holy Spirit] had never yet lived/manifested 'through' them — therefore, he did not 'know' them, yet.)* And so, Jesus told them again to be prepared, always — because, they never know when the Son of man will come for them. And he told them again the parable of the wicked servant who hid his master's wealth safely in his own pocket instead of using it to increase his master's wealth *(which was symbolic of the mistake the leaders of Israel had made).* — **(Matt 25:1-30)**

Jesus said that when the Son of man returns *(with all the Holy angels — to initiate the 'Tribulations Period' and to harvest the 144,000/Remnant of Israel);* at the end of that time, he shall sit upon the throne of his glory *(upon Mount Zion; for the next 1,000 years)*. And all the nations shall be gathered before him. And he shall separate them one from another, like a shepherd divides the sheep from the goats. And he will set all the good sheep at his right hand *(Christianized mankind)*. And he will set all the rebellious goats at his left hand *(non-Christian mankind)*. Then will he say to the sheep *(the faithful and gentle)* on his right; "Come, you blessed ones of my Father; inherit the kingdom prepared for you from the foundation of the world. This; because when I was hungry you fed me, and when I was thirsty you gave me drink, and when I was a stranger you took me in, and when I was naked you clothed me, and when I was sick you visited me, and when I was in prison you came to me." And the righteous of Israel will ask him; "But, Lord — when did we do all these things for you?" And he will say; "When you did it for the least one of these, my brethren, you did it for me." Next, he will tell those wicked goats *(the selfish and cruel)* at his left hand; "Depart from me, you cursed ones; into everlasting fire, prepared for the Devil and his angels — for, you refused to extend these kindnesses to my brethren." And, so; Jesus taught in the Temple during the day — then, retired to Bethany (in the Mount of Olives). — *(See; Fig. 1 [pg. 178]).* — **(Matt 25:31-46 & Luke 21:37)**

Early in the morning (of that same day; daytime following evening), all the people came to hear Jesus teach in the Temple. Having finished telling the people so many things, Jesus now told his disciples that after two more days was the Feast of the Passover — and he was about to be betrayed unto crucifixion. Now, as Jesus sat at lunch in Bethany, in the home of Simon the Leper *(possibly, the father of Mary and Martha and Lazarus)* — in came Mary (the Magdalene), having an alabaster box of very precious ointment, and poured it on Jesus' head — *(See; Fig. 1 [pg. 178]).* *(This was now the third time that Mary anointed Jesus; the first two times, she anointed his feet.)* And again, some of the disciples were indignant; seeing only a waste of valuable resources. But Jesus told them again to leave her alone; he said that Mary was anointing him against the day of his burial.

Now, as it happened; the Chief Priests and Lawyers and Elders of Israel were assembled together at the palace of the High Priest, striving for some way to take Jesus and kill him — when (having been preordained by the scriptures that one of his own should betray him) in walked Judas Iscariot (under the influence of Satan) before the assembly of the Elders — and asked them; "What will you give me if I deliver Jesus to you?" And they quickly agreed with him for thirty pieces of silver. And from the moment Judas transacted for Jesus' betrayal, he sought for an opportunity to betray Jesus — *(See; Fig. 1 [pg. 178])*.

− (Matt 26:1-16 & Mark 14:1-11 & Luke 21:38−22:6)

*(ONE DAY before CRUCIFIXION; beginning at 6:00 p.m.):

When evening fell, certain Greeks (being among those who had come up to worship God at the Feast of the Passover) came to Philip *(in Bethany)* and requested an audience with Jesus — *(See; Fig. 1 [pg. 178])*. When Philip (and Andrew) told the message to Jesus; immediately, Jesus said; "The hour is come that the Son of man should be glorified. Here is truth: except a corn of wheat fall into the ground and die, it will remain alone. But, if it dies *(and is planted)*, it will bring forth much fruit." Then he began to tell his disciples that every man who loves his earthly life *(strives to keep it)*, will lose it.

And every man who hates his earthly life *(willingly to give it up)*, will receive eternal life. And he told them that any man who wishes to serve him must be willing to follow in his footsteps — because, wherever Jesus is *(performer of Goodness & Truth)*, there will his true servant be *(performer of Goodness & Truth)*, also. And he promised them that his Father will honor any man who is willing to serve him *(in Goodness and Truth)*. — *(John 12:20-26)*

And then Jesus confided in his disciples, saying; "Now, my soul is troubled. And what shall I say — 'Father, save me from this hour'? Heaven forbid; it was for this cause *(dying)* that I have come unto this hour. 'Father, glorify your name'." Just then, a voice was heard out of heaven, saying; "I have both glorified it, and will glorify it, again." And the people that stood by heard it. Some heard it only as thunder. But others heard the words and thought that an angel spoke to him. And Jesus told them that the voice had not come for his benefit — but for their sakes. And he explained that now is the judgment of the world — and now shall the prince of the world be cast out. He said; "If I be lifted up from the earth,

I will draw all men to myself." (He said this, signifying by what death he should die.) And the people said to him; "The Law says that Christ lives forever — but you speak that the 'Son of Man' must be raised up — who is this Son of man?" And Jesus told them; "The light is only with you for a little while. Walk while you have light, lest the darkness come upon you — because, those who walk in darkness don't know where they're going. While you have light, believe in the light; so that you may be children of the light." And when Jesus finished speaking all these things, he hid himself from the multitudes *(speaking only to his disciples, thereafter)* — *(See; Fig. 1 [pg. 178])*. —

(John 12:27-36)

And even though Jesus had done so many miracles before the people, many of them still did not believe on him — just as it was written by the prophet, Isaiah; "Lord, who has believed our testimony? And to whom has the arm of the Lord been revealed?" - And; "He has blinded their eyes, and hardened their heart; that they should not see with their eyes, nor understand with their heart and be converted, and I should heal them." These things Isaiah spoke, when he saw Christ's glory and spoke of him. Therefore, because some *(leaders of Judaism)* were blinded, they could not believe. Nevertheless, even some of the chief rulers of Israel believed on Jesus. But, for fear of the Pharisees, they did not confess Jesus, aloud (lest they be cast out of the Synagogues). For these men loved the praise of their fellow man more than the praise of God. Therefore, was their salvation lost to them; because they would not confess, aloud, that Jesus was the Son of God. Jesus cried as he told the disciples; "He that believes on me, believes not on me, but on He that sent me. And he that sees me, sees Him that sent me. I *(the Word)* am come, a light unto the world — that whoever believes on me should no longer live in darkness. And if any man hears my Words and does not believe; I don't judge him. I came to save the world, not to judge it. He that rejects me and my Words already has someone to judge him; the Words which I have spoken — they will judge him, in the last day. For these aren't my Words which I have spoken to you; the Father who sent me commanded me to speak everything I have spoken to you. And I know that

His commandment is life everlasting *(eternal truth).*"
- *(John 12:37-50)*

   And when daylight dawned *(of the same day;
daytime following evening)*, the disciples asked Jesus
where they should prepare for him to eat his Passover
meal — *(See; Fig. 1 [pg. 178])*. *(Now, if the blood of
Jesus was to cover mankind on Passover Day — Jesus,
becoming our 'Passover lamb' — then, Jesus would [of
necessity] have to be 'dead' on Passover day [the day
of the Passover Feast]. However — as a Jew himself,
Jesus was required [by Jewish Law] to participate in
the Feast of the Passover at some other point during
Passover week if he knew he wouldn't be able to
participate on the day of Passover [according to
Numbers 9:9-12]. That being the case; Jesus chose to
eat his Passover Feast [the 'Last Supper'] one day
early — with his disciples.)* And, so; Jesus sent Peter
and John to speak to a certain man in Jerusalem,
saying; "The Master says, my time is at hand; I will
keep the Passover at your house with my disciples."
And when the man had agreed, they prepared Jesus'
Passover Supper, there — in a large upper room — *(See;*

Fig. 1 [pg. 178]). — **(Matt 26:17-19 & Mark 14:12-16 &**

Luke 22:7-13)

CHAPTER 5 — THE LAST SUPPER

*(CRUCIFIXION day):

And when the hour reached 6:00 p.m. *(the beginning of Crucifixion Day)*, Jesus and the disciples sat down together, to eat the Last Supper. *(For all the rest of the Jews, the Passover Feast would take place tomorrow, at 6:00 p.m.)* — **(Matt 26:20 & Mark 14:17 & Luke 22:14)**

(Again: On the Hebrew calendar [beginning at Gen 1:4-5], a 'day' consisted of twelve hours of darkness [first], followed by twelve hours of daylight. This is opposite of what modern man considers a 'day'. Jesus' Last Supper began at 6:00 o'clock in the evening, on the very same day (24-hour period) that he would be

hung on the cross [at 9:00 o'clock in the morning];
daytime following evening].)

    As Jesus sat down to eat with the Twelve Apostles
(and [doubtless] Lazarus; who, had been eating at the
table with Jesus and the disciples ever since his
resurrection [John 12:2]), Jesus said to them; "Here
is truth: one of you will betray me." And when his
disciples heard this, they were heartbroken. Each one
began to ask Jesus; "Is it I, Lord?" And Jesus
answered them; "It is one of the Twelve; one that dips
his hand with me in the dish." *(I believe Jesus'*
answer clearly indicates the presence of at least one
other [non-apostle] person seated at the table with
Jesus and the twelve. Why else would Jesus answer, 'It
is one of the twelve'? There is no logical reason why
Lazarus wouldn't have been present and seated with
them.) Then Jesus told them; "The Son of man will
depart, as it is written of him — but woe to the man
by whom the Son of man is betrayed; he would have been
better off if he had never been born." Then Jesus
picked up the bread and blessed it, and brake it. And
he gave the pieces of it to the disciples, saying;
"Take and eat it; this bread is my body; which, is

given for you. Do this, to remember me." *(These Words
— given to us by Jesus, at the Last Supper — are the
verses upon which the Christian sacrament of
'Communion' is based. Here; the bread is symbolic of
the Word of God [the Old and New Testament
scriptures]. The breaking of the bread is symbolic of
the Body of Christ being broken to pay our sin debt
[so that we may be redeemed by his blood]. We must eat
this 'bread'/Word daily [spiritual Communion], in
order to remember him — because, if we stop eating it,
his Word will fade away from us. We must, also,
sacramentally provide the outward 'display' [physical
Communion] of this truth — for the whole world to see
— so that others can come to understand the purpose of
Jesus' great sacrifice for us, through our example.)*
Then, Jesus picked up his cup *(of wine)* and gave
thanks. And, passing it to his disciples, he told
them; "Take this and divide it among yourselves *(pass
it from one sanctified Christian to the next)*. Drink
all of it. This cup is the New Testament in my blood
(symbolic of his Holy-Spirit blood), which is shed for
you for the remission of sins." *(Contrary to the
'bread' symbolism of the Word — which, we must 'chew*

on', to reap benefit from — the 'cup' symbolizes the Holy Spirit of Truth [which, we simply 'drink in' as we read the Word and commune with God; no chewing required].) And Jesus told his disciples; "With passion, I have desired to eat this Passover with you, before I suffer. And I will not eat again until all be fulfilled in the Kingdom of God. And I will not drink of the fruit of the vine, until I drink it new with you, in the Kingdom of God." — **(Matt 26:21-29 & Mark 14:18-25 & Luke 22:15-22)**

And as they ate, the disciples began to question among themselves which disciple would betray Jesus. And there was also a strife among them; who should be accounted 'greatest' among them. But again Jesus told them that even though the kings of the Gentiles exercise lordship over their people, Christians shall not be like them — but rather; the greatest among the body of Christ should be a 'servant' to the Christian body. And he used himself as an example, asking them; "Who is greater; he who sits at supper...or, he that serves supper?" And answering his own question, he said; "It is the one who sits and eats — and yet, I am also among you as one who serves." — **(Luke 22:23-27)**

And when they had finished eating, Jesus sat reflecting: He had loved his own that were in the world — right up to the end. He knew that the Devil had already put it in the heart of Judas Iscariot to betray him, and that his hour had finally come to depart from the world. He knew that he had come forth from God and would return to God — and that the Father had given all things into his hands. Knowing all these things, therefore; Jesus arose from the table and laid his garments aside, and took a towel and wrapped it around himself. And he poured water into a basin and began to wash the feet of his disciples — drying them off with the towel that he wore around his waist. And when he came to Peter, Peter refused to allow Jesus to wash his feet. But Jesus told Peter that if he refused to let Jesus wash his feet, then he was refusing Jesus. Therefore, did Peter immediately repent, telling him; "Lord, wash not my feet only, but also my hands and my head." But Jesus explained; "He who is 'clean' *(saved)* needs only to wash his feet, thereafter *(in other words; 'You have already been bought out of the death-sentence of sin — now, you only have to ask forgiveness [and be forgiven] any*

time you may trip up, and sin). And you are all clean,
except one *(this, because he knew who would betray
him)*." — *(John 13:1-11)*

And after Jesus had finished washing their feet,
he put his own garments back on and sat back down with
them at the table. And he said, to them; "Do you
understand what I just did to you? You call me
'Master' and 'Lord' — and you say well; for, I am your
Lord and Master. And if I, being your master, have
washed your feet — understand, thereby, that you also
should wash one another's feet *(forgive one another)*;
for, I have given you the example. Here is truth: the
servant is not greater than his Lord — nor, is that
one who is sent, greater than the one who sent him."
Jesus told them that if they can understand and accept
that it is God's will for them to be 'servants' in the
earth, they will be much happier as they serve.
(Although, he knew this knowledge would not help all
of them to serve with a sacrificial heart — because,
Jesus knew which ones he had chosen, and which one had
chosen him.) He told them the scripture must be
fulfilled (which said, 'He that eats bread with me has
lifted up his heel against me'.) And he said it, so

that when it comes to pass, they would remember this prophecy, too — and it might further solidify their belief that he is the Messiah. — *(John 13:12-19)*

Then Jesus said; "Here is truth: whoever receives the (Christian) I send, receives me. And he that receives me receives him that sent me." And as the words came out of his mouth, Jesus was immediately troubled in his spirit — and he mentioned, again; "One of you will betray me." Then they began to look each other over, again — doubting of whom he spoke. Now, the 'disciple whom Jesus loved' was leaning on Jesus breast, at that moment. *(Some people believe this disciple was John — but, others believe him to have been Lazarus.)* In any event; Peter, taking notice of him, beckoned to him that he should ask Jesus who it was that would betray him. And (lying on Jesus breast) that disciple did ask Jesus. And he answered; "It is he to whom I shall give a sop, when I have dipped it." And when he dipped the sop, he gave it to Judas Iscariot. After the sop, Satan entered into Judas, and Jesus told him; "That thing which you are willing to do — do it quickly." — *(John 13:20-27)*

Now, no man at the table understood what Jesus was saying, to Judas. But, immediately after receiving the sop, Judas went out, on his way. And it was dark outside *(probably 9:00 or 10:00 p.m.)*. And once Judas had gone his way, Jesus said to the disciples; "Now is the Son of man glorified — and God is glorified, in him. And if God is glorified in him, God shall also glorify him in himself — and soon." And he told the disciples that since they have remained with him throughout his temptations, he has appointed a kingdom unto them (such as his Father has appointed unto him) so, that they may eat and drink at his table in the Kingdom of Heaven and sit on thrones judging the twelve tribes of Israel. He told them; "Little children, I will only be with you a little while longer. You will seek me, and like I told the Jews; where I go, ye cannot come *(yet)*. So, now I give you a new commandment; that you love one another as I have loved you. By this, all men shall know that you are my disciples; if you have love one toward another." —
(Luke 22:28-30 & John 13:28-35)

And Simon (Peter) asked Jesus; "Lord, where do you go?" And Jesus answered him; "Where I go, you cannot follow me now. But you shall follow me, afterwards." And Jesus said to him; "Simon, Satan has desired to have you — that he may sift you as wheat. But I have prayed for you; that your faith will not fail you. And when you are converted *(fully 'sanctified' in the Holy Ghost [at Pentecost])*, strengthen your brethren *('tend the flock')*." And Simon (Peter) asked Jesus why he couldn't follow him, now...proclaiming to Jesus that he would willingly go to prison — or, even die for Jesus — right now. And Jesus told him gently; "Peter, Here is truth: this night — before the cock crows — you will deny even knowing me, three times." Then Jesus said to the disciples; "Do you remember when I sent you out in pairs of two — without purse, or scrip, or shoes? Did you lack anything?" And they answered; "No — nothing." And Jesus said; "From this time, forward, I say that if you have a purse *(financial resources)*, take it with you — and likewise; scrip *(supplies to write with)*. And if you do not have a sword *(a battle weapon)*, sell your clothing and buy one *(also see; Exo 22:2-3, Neh 4:14, Est 8:11-12 & 9:1-5)* — for, I tell you; the prophecy which is written must yet be accomplished, in me; which said, 'And he was reckoned among the transgressors' *(in other words; even Jesus was abused as if he were evil, rather than good)*. For, the things concerning me have an end." And they said; "Lord, here are two swords." And Jesus said; "It is enough." *(I have personally never heard a sermon addressing this particular passage, where Jesus appears to be telling his disciples [faithful & gentle 'sheep'] to arm themselves with swords and prepare to fight. Could he have been eluding to the 'sword of the Lord' [the Word] — as if saying, 'Trade everything you have, for the Word of God'?].)* — **(Matt 26:31-35, Mark 14:27-31, Luke 22:31-38 & John 13:36-38)**

Then, Jesus said to his disciples; "Let not your hearts be troubled; you believe in God — believe also in me *(have faith in me)*. In my Father's house are many mansions. I go there, to prepare a place for you. And if I go to prepare a place for you, I will come back to collect you — that where I am, there you may be also. And you know where I go — and you know the way." But Thomas said to him; "Lord, we don't know where you're going — and how can we know the way?" And Jesus told him; "I am the way; the truth and the light. No man can come to the Father, except by me. If you know me *(if Christ lives inside you and manifests through you)*, you know my Father also *(Goodness & Truth, the Father)* — and from henceforth, you do know him and have seen him." Then Philip said to Jesus; "Lord, show us the Father and we will be content." But Jesus said to him; "Have I been with you such a long time, Philip, and still you haven't 'known' me? He that has seen me has seen the Father. Do you not believe that I am in the Father, and the Father in me? The Words that I speak are not mine, but the Father's (who dwells in me); He does the works *(the miracles; the increase)*. Either believe that the Father and I are one, or, believe me for the very works' sake *(the results you have seen)*." — *(John 14:1-11)*

And he said; "Here is truth: he who believes on me; these works that I do, he shall do, too. And greater works than these will he do, because I go to my Father. And whatever you ask in my name *('Savior)*, I will do it; so that my Father may be glorified in the Son. If you love me, keep my commandments. And I will pray to the Father so that He will give you another comforter to abide with you forever; the

Spirit of Truth (whom, the rest of the world cannot receive because they don't see him, or, know him). But you 'know' him because he dwells with you and shall be inside you. I will not leave you comfortless; I *(Christ; the Holy Spirit of Truth)* will come to you. Very soon, the world will see me no more. But, you see me. Because I live, you shall also live. On that day, you will know that I am in my Father, and you are in me — and I am in you. He that has my commandments, and keeps *(studies/obeys/proclaims)* them, loves me. And he that loves me shall be loved of my Father. I will love that one and will manifest myself to him *(the Holy Spirit will manifest through that one)*." — *(John 14:12-21)*

Then, Judas (not Iscariot) said to him; "Lord, how will you manifest yourself to us but not to the world?" And Jesus told him; "If a man loves me, he will keep my Words — and my Father will love him. And we will come and live inside of him. But he that doesn't love me will not keep *(study/obey/proclaim)* my Words *(he will never have that 'reserve', to draw from)*. These Words that you hear from me are not mine; they are the Words of the Father who sent me. All these things I have spoken, being yet present with you (in the flesh). But the comforter (which is the Holy Ghost; the Spirit of Truth) whom the Father will send to (live inside) you, in my name — He shall teach you all things, and bring to your remembrance every Word that I have spoken to you. Peace I leave with you; my peace, I give to you. Not as the world gives peace, do I give it. Let not your heart be troubled, nor, afraid. You are worried that I said, 'I go away, and will return again, to you'. But if you love me, you should rejoice that I say I go unto my Father — because my Father is greater than me. And I have foretold you all these things so that when they come to pass you might believe." Then Jesus said; "I won't talk much with you after this, because the prince of this world is coming — and he has nothing in me. But; so that the world may know I love the Father, I do exactly as the Father has commanded me." And after they had sung an hymn, Jesus said; "Arise, and let us go (to the Mount of Olives)." And they left the upper room, to go to the Garden — (See; Fig. 1 [pg. 178]). — **(Luke 22:39 & John 14:22-31 (& Matt 26:30 & Mark 14:26, out of sequence)**

And as Jesus walked with his disciples that evening to the Garden of Gethsemane, he spoke much to them about how the Kingdom of God grows through divine love and sacrifice. He explained that he himself is the 'true vine' — and Christians are the branches on his vine *(each new branch becoming a part of the growing Body of Christ)*. He explained that the function and purpose of each branch is to bear fruit *(the fruit of the Holy Spirit; Goodness & Truth)* — and therefore, they need to understand that God will cut off every branch which does not produce fruit (observing that branch to be 'dead'). Jesus told his disciples that each Christian is clean 'through' the Word that he has spoken to them *(which they must keep flowing through them; retaining it in their knowledge and proclaiming it to the world)* — *(this is the divine blood that flows through their souls, now; connecting them to God and to Jesus)*. In other words; only if they continue to live in his Word will they continue to be able to produce his fruit. Jesus told them that as long as his blood flows through them; anything they ask in his name *('Savior')*, they would receive. *(I understand this verse to be saying that anything they ask in the name of 'saving'/strengthening the Kingdom of God, they will receive.)* He explained that just as the Father loves him, he loves all of them — and if they will continue to keep his commandments *(study/obey/proclaim them)*, he and the Father would continue to love them, and his Word-blood would continue to be theirs. He explained all this, so that their joy *(their 'glory')* might remain, and be full. — **(Luke 22:39 & John 15:1-11)**

Then, Jesus told them; "This is my commandment; that you love one another as I have loved you *(which means; 'sacrificially')*." He told them; "Greater love has no man, than that he would give up his own life for his friends. You are my friends — if you do what I command you." Therefore, Jesus explained that he no longer considers them 'servants' — but rather; 'friends' (because; whereas a servant isn't made privy to his master's business, Jesus has revealed to these disciples all things that his Father ever spoke to him). He told them they did not choose him — but rather; he chose them (and ordained them, to go and bring forth more fruit — and that their fruit would remain). Jesus told them that if the world hates them, now; they should find comfort in knowing that it hated him, first. He said that if they were 'of' the world, the world would love its own. But because he has chosen them 'out' of the world, that's why the world hates them, now. Jesus said that if the world first persecuted him, it will also persecute them. And if good people have kept Jesus' Words, they will also keep his disciples. But, either way; it's all being done for his name's sake. Jesus said he was telling them all these harsh truths so that they would not be surprised or offended when they were put out of the Synagogues. And he said the time was coming when everyone who kills a Christian will think he's doing God a service — but it will be because they have never known the Father *(Goodness & Truth)*, or, the Son *(Goodness & Truth)*. — *(John 15:12—16:3)*

Then, Jesus told them; "Now, I go my way to Him that sent me — and sorrow has filled your hearts. I tell you the truth; it is expedient *(beneficial)* for you that I go. For, if I don't go, the Comforter will not come into you *(Jesus' body had to be broken/killed, for the Holy Spirit to be released into the world)*." He added; "And when he does enter into you *(inside your heart)*, he will reprove the world of sin, and of righteousness, and of judgment." And he told them; "I have so many things to say to you — but you cannot bear them now *(they will come, later; after his death/resurrection)*. And, when the Holy Spirit of Truth is come into you, he *(the Voice of God)* will guide you into all truth; he *(Christ)* will speak the Words of God to you, and show you all things to come. Soon, you will not see me — and then after a little while, you will see me again; because I go to the Father." Then some of his disciples talked among themselves — trying to figure out what Jesus meant by all these things. And Jesus knew they were confused, so he told them; "Ye shall weep and lament — but be patient; your sorrow will be turned into joy. When a woman is in labor, she has sorrow (because of the pain). But as soon as she delivers the child, she no longer remembers the anguish — for the joy that a new life has entered the world. Your heart will rejoice — and no man can take your joy away. In that day, all of your questions will be answered. And whatever you ask in my name *('Savior')* the Father will give it to you. Up till now, you haven't been able to ask 'in my name'

(as a 'savior') — but then, you will be able to; so
that your joy *(your glory)* may be full." **- (John 16:4-24)**

And Jesus told them; "All these things, I have
spoken to you in proverbs — but the time is coming
when I shall show you plainly of the Father. On that
day, you will ask what you will — in my name
('Savior') — and the Father *(Goodness & Truth)* Himself
will hear you; because you have believed that I came
forth from Him, and He loves you, for it." And his
disciples said to Jesus; "We believe that you came
forth from God." And Jesus said; "Do you? The hour has
come that you will be scattered; every man to his own
— leaving me alone. And yet, I am not alone; because
the Father *(Goodness & Truth)* is with me. I speak
these things, so that you may have peace *(when you
abandon me, in fear)*. In the world, you will have
tribulation. But be of good cheer; I have overcome the
world." **- (John 16:25-33)**

And as Jesus neared the Garden of Gethsemane,
with his disciples, he lifted his eyes to heaven and
began to pray. He asked his Father to glorify His Son;
so that His Son could glorify Him. Jesus had given the

Word of God to the world — and God's children were able to believe that he is the Son of God, through his Word. And Jesus didn't ask God to rescue his children out of the world, right then. Instead; he asked that God would 'keep' the children from evil, while they must yet remain on the earth *(to bring many sons to glory)*. He asked his Father to sanctify his children through the truth of His Word *(through the Holy Spirit of Truth)*. He prayed, not only for the brethren he was leaving behind — but also for all those Christians who would be born afar off. He asked his Father to *(one day)* bring all of his brethren to be with him, where he is. All these things, Jesus asked; so that the same love the Father loves him with, may be in all of his children — and Jesus, in them. — *(John 17:1-26)*

And when Jesus had spoken these words to his disciples, they went forth over the brook Cedron, where was the Garden of Gethsemane; into which, they entered — *(See; Fig. 1 [pg. 178])*. And the garden was a place known to Judas Iscariot; for Jesus often came here to relax with the disciples. And just inside the garden, Jesus asked the disciples to sit down — but, he took Peter and James and John a little further into the garden, with him. And his countenance became very heavy. And he told these three; "My soul is exceedingly sorrowful, even unto death *(foreknowing everything that he was about to suffer)*. Wait here, and watch with me. And pray; so that you enter into no temptation." And Jesus left them — walking about a stone's throw away — and fell on his face, to pray — saying; "Father, all things are possible to you; if it be possible, take away this cup from me. Nevertheless — not my will, but yours, be done." And then he returned again to Peter, James and John — and he found them sleeping. He said to Peter; "Could you not watch with me, for one hour? Watch and pray; so that you enter not into temptation! The spirit indeed is willing, but the flesh is weak." **— (Matt 26:36-41 & Mark 14:32-38 & Luke 22:40-42 & John 18:1-2)**

Then Jesus went away again the second time, and prayed; saying; "O my Father; if this cup may not pass away from me, except I drink it — thy will be done." And he returned again to the three disciples — and again found them asleep *(for their eyes were very heavy, and they knew no words to comfort Jesus)*. So, Jesus went away again the third time; and prayed the same words. And being in agony, he prayed the more earnestly — and his sweat was like great drops of blood falling down to the ground. *(This is an actual medical condition that exists even today; wherein, extreme stress causes the blood to evacuate the body with profuse perspiration.)* And there appeared to him an angel from heaven; to give him strength. And when he rose up from praying, he returned again to the three, and found them asleep again. Then Jesus said; "Take your rest; it is enough. The hour is come. The Son of man is betrayed into the hands of sinners." And even as Jesus yet spoke, in came Judas Iscariot into the garden — with a band of men and officers from the Chief Priests and Pharisees of Israel, carrying lanterns and torches and weapons; for to take Jesus. — *(Matt 26:42-47 & Mark 14:39-43 & Luke 22:43-47 & John 18:3)*

Now, Judas had given the Pharisees a sign, saying; "Whomsoever I kiss; that man is Jesus." Therefore, did Judas immediately come forward, saying; "Hail Master," and kissed Jesus. And Jesus said to him; "Judas, do you betray the Son of man with a kiss *(of all things)*?" And knowing everything that must come upon him; Jesus went forth to the multitude and asked them; "Whom do you seek?" And they answered him; "Jesus of Nazareth." And Jesus said; "I am he." And the men went backward, and fell to the ground. Jesus asked them again; "Whom do you seek?" They answered; "Jesus of Nazareth." And Jesus said; "I told you that I am he — therefore, let these others go their way." And when they moved to lay hands on Jesus, Peter drew out a sword and chopped off the ear of one of the High Priest's servants (and the servant's name was Malchus). Then said Jesus to Peter; "Put away your sword. Shall I not drink the cup my Father has given me to drink? And *(by the way)* every man who takes up the sword, shall die with the sword. Do you think I can't pray my Father, and he should immediately give me more than twelve legions of angels? But, how then shall the scriptures be fulfilled; which, say it must be this way?" And Jesus touched the ear of Malchus, and healed him. *(This is an interesting turn of events — since Jesus had just warned them, hours earlier, that if they didn't have a sword they should go sell their clothes and buy one. But surely this verse is proof that he wasn't referring to an actual sword, when he said that.)* Then Jesus said to the multitude of men; "Are you come out against me as a thief; with swords and staves, to take me? I was daily with you in the Temple teaching, and you did not take me. But this is your hour (and the hour of darkness); the scriptures must be fulfilled." – *(Matt 26:48-55 & Mark 14:44-49 & Luke 22:47-53 & John 18:4-11)*

And when they laid hands on Jesus, all of his disciples forsook him in fear, and fled away *(just as Jesus told them they would)*. And as they led Jesus away, bound, there followed him a certain young man (wearing a linen cloth around his naked body). And one of the priests' men laid hold on him — but he slipped out of the linen cloth and fled from them, naked. *(For reasons that will not become apparent until later, I believe this young follower was Lazarus.)* And Peter, also, followed afar off. And they led Jesus away to the palace of Caiaphas (the High Priest); where the Chief Priests and Lawyers and Elders of Israel were assembled; waiting, to interrogate Jesus — *(See; Fig. 1 [pg. 178])*. And they took Jesus first to Annas (the Father-in-law of Caiaphas). (And Caiaphas was he that had given counsel to Israel that it was expedient that one man should die for the people.) Now, Peter *(a lowly fisherman)* waited outside the door of the palace, with many others. But the unnamed disciple *(the young man which had fled the guards naked, from the garden)*; he, was 'known' to the High Priest; therefore, he was allowed to go in with Jesus, into the interrogation. *(It is significant that the High Priest both 'recognizes' and 'allows' this unnamed young follower of Jesus to enter into the palace [where, only Priests and rulers [or, their servants] may have been permitted entry. Also; this young man had enough 'influence' within the palace to instruct the door attendant to permit Peter [a lowly fisherman] inside the palace, as well. It makes sense to me that this unnamed disciple was, in fact, Lazarus [the rich young ruler?] ...who, so many Jews had honored upon his death.)* Once they had kindled a fire in the hall, Peter *(the lowly fisherman)* sat down among the servants and officers, to wait. Now, as Peter sat and warmed himself by the fire, the damsel who kept the door began to recognize him, saying; "This man was also with Jesus. Aren't you one of his disciples?" But Peter denied, saying; "Woman, I do not know the man."

— (Matt 26:56-58 & Mark 14:50-54 & Luke 22:54-62 & John 18:12-18)

Meanwhile; inside the palace, they interrogated Jesus — *(See; Fig. 1 [pg. 178])*. The High Priest began by asking him about his disciples and his doctrine. But, Jesus answered; "All this time, I have spoken openly to the world — teaching in the Synagogue and in the Temple. I have said nothing in secret. Why do you ask me of my doctrine? Ask those who heard me speak." *(After all; they had presumably arrested Jesus because of what he preached.)* But because he answered the High Priest with these words, one of the officers struck Jesus. Jesus said to the man; "If I have spoken evil, bear witness of the evil. But, if I have spoken well; why do you strike me?" And a witness came forward, testifying that Jesus said he would destroy the Temple of God and rebuild it in three days — without human hands. But, no one else's story of the same account matched with his. Also, many other false witnesses began to come forward against Jesus — but all of their testimonies conflicted with one another, and the Law of Moses requires that two witnesses must agree, exactly. Therefore, the High Priest rose up and said to Jesus; "Have you nothing to say for yourself against these testimonies (hoping to entangle Jesus in his own words)?!" But Jesus held his peace. — *(Matt 26:59-63 & Mark 14:55-61 & John 18:19-24)*

And finally; the High Priest demanded of Jesus; "I adjure you, by the living God; tell us whether you are Christ, the Son of God." And Jesus answered; "If I tell you, you will not believe. And if I ask you that question, you will not answer. Nor, will you let me go, anyway. But, henceforth, you *(speaking to the evil spirits, within them)* shall see the Son of man sitting on the right hand of power, and coming in the clouds of heaven." And they demanded, again; "Are you the Son of God?!" And finally Jesus answered; "I am." Therefore; the High Priest ripped his clothes, and said to the assembly; "What further witnesses do we need? You have all heard his blasphemy. What say you?" And they answered; "He is guilty of death." Then they began to spit in Jesus' face. And they put a blindfold on him and began to strike him, saying; "Prophesy to us, Christ; which of us struck you?" — *(Matt 26:63-68 & Mark 14:61-65 & Luke 22:63-71)*

And when they had finished humiliating Jesus,
they led him away, bound, to the Hall of Judgment — to
the Governor; Pontius Pilate — *(See; Fig. 1 [pg.
178])*. Now, Peter *(who waited precariously down below,
among the servants and officers)* had fled the inner
hall when he was recognized by the damsel who kept the
door. But now — as he stood warming himself on the
porch — he was once again recognized — by a man in the
crowd. This time; his accuser spoke aloud to the
multitude, saying; "This fellow was also with Jesus of
Nazareth — and his Galilean speech gives him away."
But, Peter swore (with an oath), saying; "I do not
know the man!" But once he had been pointed out in the
crowd, Peter was quickly recognized by a relative of
Malchus *(the servant whose ear Peter cut off, in the
Garden of Gethsemane)*; which, then shouted boldly;
"Didn't I see you in the garden with Jesus?!" But,
Peter began to curse and swear — saying; "I do not
know this man of whom you speak!" And immediately, a
cock crowed; for morning had dawned *(of that same day;
daytime following evening)*. And Jesus *(who, was being
led down through the crowd at that very moment)* turned
and looked at Peter just as the cock had crowed *(Luke*

22:61) — and Peter instantly remembered the Lord's words; "Before the cock crows, you will deny me three times." Therefore, Peter ran away — and wept, bitterly. *(But thankfully, Jesus had assured Peter [hours earlier] that he would still be loved and forgiven, even after stumbling at this test of his courage.)* — **(Matt 26:69—27:1 & Mark 14:66—15:1 & Luke 22:72—23:1 & John 18:25—28)**

Meanwhile; when Judas realized that Jesus had been condemned to death *(rather than taking the throne of Israel, when his hand had been forced)*, Judas repented of betraying Jesus. So, he brought back the thirty pieces of silver, to the Chief Priests and Elders of Israel, saying; "I have sinned; betraying innocent blood." But the priests told Judas; "What do we care; that's between you and God." So, Judas threw the money at them and ran away and hanged himself. *(Sadly, the one person Judas had not confessed his sin to, was God.)* Therefore, the priests would later use that money to buy the Potter's Field — to bury strangers who might die in their city. *(And this, too, would come to pass, just as it had been foretold by prophecy; in Zechariah 11:12-13.)* And when the Elders of Israel finally arrived at the Judgment Hall with Jesus *(to deliver him to Pontius Pilate)*, they would not enter inside the hall themselves; lest they should be defiled for Passover *(seeing that their business was to seek a 'death' penalty). (You see; it was early morning, of Preparation Day; the day prior to the Annual Feast of the Passover [which, Feast, would begin at 6:00 o'clock that evening] — and the Law of Moses says that anything having to do with 'death' will defile a Jew, for Passover. For this reason, the Jews would not enter into the Hall — therefore, Pilate had to come outside the Hall to speak with the angry mob of Jewish Elders.)* When Pilate asked them what accusations had been brought against their prisoner, they answered; "We found this fellow perverting the nation of Israel, and forbidding to give tribute to Caesar *(pay taxes)* — saying that he himself is Christ (a king)." And Pilate said; "Take him and judge him according to your own law, then." But they said; "It is not lawful for us *(Jews)* to put a man to death." *(The world was under Roman rule at this time, and only Romans could execute a death penalty against an*

244

accused.) — *(Matt 27:1-10 & Mark 15:1 & Luke 23:2 &*
John 18:28-32)

So, Pilate took Jesus back into the Judgment Hall
with him, to interrogate him — saying; "So, you are
the King of the Jews?" — *(See; Fig. 1 [pg. 178])* And
Jesus asked him; "Do you say this of yourself — or,
has someone else told it to you?" And Pilate said; "Am
I a Jew?! Your own nation and Chief Priests have
delivered you to me. What have you done?" And although
the Chief Priests had accused Jesus of many things,
Jesus answered Pilate nothing. And by the end of their
discussion, Pilate himself could find no fault in
Jesus. This provoked the Jews to become even more
fierce in their accusations against Jesus — demanding;
"He stirs up the people; teaching throughout all Jewry
— from Galilee to Jerusalem." When Pilate heard them
mention Galilee, he asked them if Jesus were a
Galilean. And when the Jews confirmed that Jesus was
indeed from Galilee — a citizen belonging to the
jurisdiction of Herod, the Jewish Tetrarch — Pilate
happily sent the whole multitude to Herod *(for, Herod*
happened to be in Jerusalem at that moment). — *(Matt*
27:11-14 & Mark 15:2-5 & Luke 23:3-7 & John 18:33-35)

And when Jesus was brought before Herod, Herod was elated. He had long wanted to meet Jesus — hoping to see some miracle done by him. And Herod interviewed Jesus for a long time, as the Chief Priests and Lawyers of Israel stood vehemently accusing him — but Jesus would answer him nothing. So, Herod and his men began to provoke Jesus; they dressed him in a gorgeous robe and set him in the middle of the room and mocked him. But in the end; Herod could find nothing worthy of death in Jesus, either — and he sent him back to Pilate. — *(Luke 23:8-12)*

The second time Jesus spoke to Pilate, Jesus told him; "My kingdom is not of this world. If it were, my servants would fight to keep me from being delivered to the will of the Jews." So, Pilate said; "You are a king, then?" And Jesus said; "You say I am a king. To this end, was I born, and for this cause am I come into the world — that I should bear witness unto the truth. Everyone that is of the truth can hear my voice." (To which, the frustrated Pilate responded; "What is truth?") Just then; Pilate's wife sent word to him — warning; "Have nothing to do with that just man; for I have suffered many things this day in a dream, because of him." So, Pilate went back outside to reason with the Jews. He told them; "You brought this man to me, as one that perverts the people. I have examined him before you, and I find no fault in him regarding those things whereof you accuse him. Nor, yet, did Herod find any fault in him; for I sent you to him, and he also found nothing worthy of death, in the man. Therefore, I would chastise him and release him." He said, further; "You have a custom; that I should release one prisoner to you, at the Passover. You may have either Barabbas *(the murderer)*...or, Jesus; which is called Christ." And as Pilate returned to the judgment seat, he asked *(deliberately)*; "Are you willing that I should release to you the King of the Jews?" *(Pilate stated his question this way because he knew that it was only for envy that the Jews had delivered Jesus to him, to be executed.)* But the Jews held fast their campaign, shouting; "Give us not this man, but Barabbas!" – **(Matt 27:15-19 & Mark 15:6-11 & Luke 23:13-19 & John 18:36-39)**

Pilate was obligated to act upon the unyielding demand of the Jewish Elders — but he was still not willing to put Jesus to death. Therefore, he commanded instead to have Jesus taken and scourged by his Roman soldiers — *(See; Fig. 1 [pg. 178])*. *('Scourging' amounted to forty-nine lashes with a nine-tailed whip, having sharp barbs of bone tied at the tip of each tail; this was a torture device designed to rip chunks of flesh off of its victim)*. Pilate hoped this brutal torture would satiate the bloodthirsty crowd. But, Pilate's soldiers *(behind closed doors)* took their helpless captive even further into the abyss: After they had finished ripping the flesh off Jesus's back with their whip, the soldiers took it upon themselves to weave a crown of thorns *(from thorny branches)* and they pressed it deep into Jesus' scalp. And when they had stripped him and dressed him in a purple robe, they bowed the knee before him and mocked him — saying; "Hail, King of the Jews!" Then, they began to strike him with their open hands. Eventually, Pilate reappeared before the Jews *(thinking to make a successful appeal for Jesus' release, now)*. He said to them; "Behold; I bring him forth to you, that you may know I find no fault in him." And when the soldiers brought Jesus forward — bloody and beaten, and dressed in the crown of thorns and the purple robe — the Chief Priests and officers had no pity for Jesus, whatsoever. They cried out; "Crucify him! Crucify him!" But Pilate insisted; "Why?! What evil has he done?! You take him and crucify him! I find no fault in him." But they argued; "We have a law, and by our law, he ought to die — because he made himself the Son of God." — *(Matt 27:20-23 & Mark 15:12-14 & Luke 23:20-23 & John 19:1-7)*

Now, when Pilate heard that Jesus claimed to be the Son of God, he was all the more reluctant to crucify Jesus *(Romans believed in [and feared] many gods)*. And he went inside again, to speak to Jesus alone — asking him; "Where do you come from?" But, Jesus would not answer him. And Pilate said; "Will you not speak to me? Don't you know that I have the power to crucify you...or, set you free?" But Jesus assured him; "You could have no power at all against me, except it were given you, from above. Therefore, those who delivered me to you have the greater sin." And when Pilate returned again to the Jews, they immediately cried out; "If you let this man go, you are not Caesar's friend; whoever makes himself a king, speaks against Caesar." And when Pilate knew that he could prevail nothing (but rather; a tumult was made), he brought Jesus before the Jews again. And the soldiers brought Pilate a basin of water — and, Pilate washed his hands before the Jews, saying; "I am innocent of the blood of this just person." And the Jews answered him; "His blood be upon us and our children." Therefore, did Pilate release unto them the murderer, Barabbas. And he ordered Jesus to be crucified. And so, the soldiers took the robe off of Jesus and put his own clothes back on him — and they led him away to crucify him — *(See; Fig. 1 [pg. 178])*. — *(Matt 27:24-31 & Mark 15:15-20 & Luke 23:24-25 & John 19:8-16)*

By now, a great company of people surrounded and followed them — bewailing and lamenting Jesus, as they led him out of Jerusalem to the 'place of the skull'. But Jesus said to them; "Daughters of Jerusalem, do not weep for me — but weep for yourselves and your children *(Whereas, the Jewish Elders had just accepted responsibility for the murder of Jesus to fall upon every soul of Israel)*." He continued; "For the days are coming, when they will say, 'Blessed are the barren, and the wombs that never bare'. In that day, they will beg the mountains and hills to fall on them and cover them. For if they *(evil mankind)* do these things in a green tree *(while God is among them)* — what shall they do in the dry *(when God is not among them)*?" And they compelled a man of Cyrene (named Simon) to help Jesus carry his cross *(for, his body was weak, from torture and lack of sleep)*. And two other condemned men were led away with Jesus, to be put to death; thieves, both of them. — *(Matt 27:32 & Mark 15:21 & Luke 23:26-32 & John 19:17)*

CHAPTER 6 — THE CRUCIFIXION AND RESURRECTION OF JESUS

And when they were come to the place called Calvary and Golgotha, they offered Jesus wine vinegar to drink. And when he had tasted what it was *(fermented fruit of the vine)*, he refused to drink it. Then, the Roman soldiers stripped off all of his clothing, and they secured him to a large, wooden stake *(called; a 'cross')*; driving long nails through each of his wrists and through both of his feet. And as Jesus hung bleeding *(in agony)* on the cross, they crucified the other two thieves also; one to his right, and one to his left. And Jesus said; "Father, forgive them; for, they know not what they do." Then the Roman soldiers tore Jesus' garment into four parts

— each taking a piece. But his overcoat was woven through; from beginning to end — so, they cast lots to decide who would claim it. And it was the third hour of daylight *(about 9:00 am)* when they hung Jesus on the cross. And Pilate wrote a title on a plaque for him, and had it hung on the cross just above Jesus' head. The words were inscribed in Hebrew, Greek and Latin, saying; "Jesus of Nazareth, the King of the Jews". And the Chief Priests came and told Pilate; "Do not write 'King of the Jews'. Write 'He said; I am King of the Jews'." But Pilate told them; "What I have written, I have written." And he would not change a word. - *(Matt 27:33-38 & Mark 15:22-28 & Luke 23:33-38 & John 19:18-24)*

And there — at the foot of the cross — stood Jesus' mother, Mary and her sister...and Mary (the wife of Cleophas)...and Mary (the Magdalene). Also standing at the foot of the cross was the 'disciple whom Jesus loved'. *(Again; some believe the 'disciple whom Jesus loved' was John — but others believe that he was Lazarus.)* And as Jesus looked down upon them, from the cross — he said to his mother; "Woman, he will be your son." And to the disciple (whom he

loved), he said; "She will be your mother." (And from
that hour, the 'disciple whom Jesus loved' took Jesus'
mother into his own home; as his own mother.) And one
of the thieves which hung beside Jesus began to rail
on Jesus, saying; "If you are Christ, save yourself —
and us!" But the other thief rebuked the first,
saying; "Do you not fear God; seeing that we are about
to die (justly condemned) — whereas Jesus has
committed no sin?" And the humble thief asked Jesus to
remember him, when he comes into his kingdom. *(And
since this thief had just confessed both his sin, and
his faith in Jesus' deity and power)* Jesus was able to
assure him; "Of a truth, I can tell you today: 'You
shall be with me in paradise'." *(Now, many people
understand this verse to imply that the thief would be
in Paradise with Jesus that very day — but not even
Jesus, himself, would be in Paradise the very day of
his death. Jesus would first spend three days in the
bowels of the earth [Matt 12:40] and then announce to
the women at the tomb [four days after his burial]
that he had [still] not yet ascended to his father
[John 20:17]. In fact; Jesus would spend a total of 40
days 'appearing' to his disciples on the earth, before*

finally ascending into Heaven [Luke 24:46-51]. The fact that no punctuation appears in the language of the original Greek text could account for this confusion in the English translations.) (Also; the fact that this thief was never water-baptized before he died [as required, by John's Word from God] didn't prohibit his salvation. As John testified, water-baptism was performed so that the Son of God could 'manifest' to a man [perform, through him] — but this thief would not live on [to manifest any fruit] after the moment of his repentance and redemption. Neither, was his lack of water-baptism an act of disobedience. All these facts comprise the truth of the matter — and God deals with man, in truth.) **— (Luke 23:39-43 & John 19:25-27)**

And there were also enemies of Jesus, who — as they passed in front of the cross — looked up at Jesus and reviled him; wagging their heads and saying things, like; "You, who will 'destroy the Temple and raise it again in three days' — save yourself,"...and, "If you are the Son of God, come down from the cross." And the Chief Priests and Lawyers and Elders of Israel said to the crowd; "He saved others, but he cannot save himself? If he comes down from the cross we will believe that he is the Son of God. Let God deliver him; if He will have him — having claimed to be His Son." — *(Matt 27:39-44 & Mark 15:29-32)*

And, from the sixth hour of daylight *(noon)* until the ninth hour *(3:00 p.m.)* — as Jesus hang there in torment, drawing slowly nearer to death — a gloomy darkness came over the land. Then, Jesus cried out suddenly, with a loud voice; "Eli, Eli, lama sabachthani?" *(in other words; "My God, my God — why have you forsaken me?") (Jesus' sense of aloneness, in that moment, was excruciating. That Jesus must 'die the death of a transgressor' meant that he would have to die separated from his Father — and, so he would. I often wonder, when I read this passage, if this may have been another one of those details that Jesus was not made privy to, in advance [as in Mark 13:32]. I wonder if advance knowledge that he would have to be separated from God [even for a moment] would have made the mission too much for Jesus to bear [see; John 8:29]).* Afterward, Jesus (knowing that all things were now accomplished, that the scripture might be fulfilled) said; "I thirst." *(I also wonder if it was for the Holy Spirit, that he thirsted, when he said these words.)* Nevertheless; someone hurried to fill a sponge with vinegar and put it on hyssop, so that it may be lifted up to Jesus' lips. But, others in the crowd (thinking Jesus had called out to Elias, to help him) said; "Stop! Let it be! Let us see whether Elias will come to save him." And as they watched and waited, Jesus spoke out again [with his last, dying breath], saying; "Father, into your hands I commend my spirit. It is finished." And Jesus bowed his head in death, and released the Holy Ghost *(into the world)* — *(See; Fig. 1 [pg. 178])*. **- (Matt 27:45-50 & Mark 15:33-37 & Luke 23:44 & John 19:28-30)**

And when Jesus spoke those words — "It is finished" — the veil of the Temple *(in Jerusalem)* began to rip itself in half, from the top to the bottom. In this manner, did God confirm that the wall between God and man had been destroyed. Just then, the earth began to quake, violently — so, that the rocks broke apart. And, many graves were opened. *(Three days later [during Jesus' own resurrection] many bodies of the Saints which had slept in their graves would be seen walking around in the Holy City [Jerusalem], appearing to many of the people [Matt 27:52-53].)* Standing afar off — watching the chaos of these violent acts of nature — were Mary (the Magdalene)...and Mary (the mother of Jesus and James)...and Salome *(women who had ministered to Jesus; travelling with him from Galilee)* and many other women which came up with him, to Jerusalem. And when the Roman Centurion observed everything that was happening, he glorified God — saying aloud; "Surely, this was a righteous man." And many people came running to Golgotha to see what was happening — but they ran away again; for fear. **— (Matt 27:51-56 & Mark 15:38-41 & Luke 23:45-49)**

(Now, Jesus died at roughly 3:00 p.m. on a Wednesday afternoon — (See; Fig. 1 [pg. 178]). Again; according to the Hebrew Calendar, each new day begins at 6:00 p.m. — therefore; within three hours of Jesus' 3:00 o'clock death, 'Wednesday' would turn into 'Thursday' ['Preparation day' would turn into 'Passover day'] — and the Jews were not allowed to handle a dead body on Passover day [because 'death' defiles a holy day]. Therefore, the Jews needed Jesus to die and be buried before 6:00 o'clock.) That being

the case; while they had been *(impatiently)* waiting
for Jesus to die *(time, creeping ever closer to the
six o'clock hour [of Passover])* the Jews had rushed,
again, to appear before Pilate — this time; requesting
to have the three crucified men taken down from their
crosses, and their deaths 'hurried-along' by the
breaking of their legs *(so they might bleed to death,
quickly — whereas, crucifixion was a long, slow
death)*. But the Jews had no sooner made this grizzly
request of Pilate, than two other men burst into the
presence of Pilate *(Joseph and Nicodemus; secret
disciples of Jesus)* asking permission to take down the
dead body of Jesus, for burial. Learning that Jesus
had already died, Pilate was willing to let his
friends claim his body, for burial — so, he gave them
leave. He sent his soldiers along, to verify that
Jesus was, in fact, dead — and to break the legs of
the two thieves *(as the Jews had requested)*. With a
spear, the Roman soldiers pierced Jesus in his side
and testified that blood and water issued forth from
the wound. Then, they took the Lord's body down from
the cross and they gave him into the hands of Joseph
and Nicodemus. These, anointed his body with Myrrh and

Aloes and wrapped him in fine linen. And they laid him to rest in Joseph's own tomb (which he had hewn into a rock, there in the Garden). And Mary *(the Magdalene)* and Mary *(Jesus' mother)* watched, as they buried Jesus — *(See; Fig. 1 [pg. 178])*. And finally, it was 6:00 p.m.; the hour of the Passover Feast. And a certain man bear record of these events (writing them in the book we call the 'Gospel of John'). *(Unfortunately, none of the four Gospels of the New Testament were signed by their author. Attributing the credit to Matthew, Mark, Luke and John was simply mankind's best educated guess at the time those designations were assigned. For reasons that may become more apparent as we continue through the text, I am inclined to believe that the Gospel of John was actually written by Lazarus.)* And here *(in the Gospel of John)*, the Bible states; "We know his *(the author's)* record is true, and he bear record so that we might believe." *(And all these things came to pass just as they had been foretold by prophecy; in Psalm 34:20 & Zechariah 12:10)* — **(Matt 27:57-61 & Mark 15:42-47 & Luke 23:50-55 & John 19:31-42)**

Now, the Jews remained very concerned that Jesus had claimed *(in life)* that he would be resurrected by the hand of God after spending three days in the bowels of the earth *(Matt 12:40)*. And they knew that if *(in conjunction with the hour that Jesus had been buried)* his body were to 'miraculously' disappear from the grave near 6:00 p.m. on Sunday Evening, it would prove to the world that Jesus was the Messiah — *(See; Fig. 2 [pg. 261])*. Therefore; the Elders of Israel went again to Pilate. This time, they said; "We remember the deceiver said he would rise from the grave after three days. Command, therefore, that the tomb be guarded during that time; so that his disciples don't' come by night and steal away his body and tell the people that he is risen from the dead — making the last error worse than the first." And Pilate told them; "Very well; you have your guards. Go and make it as sure as you can." And so, they posted a guard of Roman soldiers by the stone that sealed the grave of Jesus. *(Nevertheless; three nights later, Jesus would be resurrected from the grave [by the hand of God], right on schedule.)* — *(See; Fig. 2, below)* — **(Matt 27:62-66)**

(Fig. 2 -- Crucifixion Week):

**(On the Hebrew Calendar, each new 'day' begins at 6:00 p.m. [not, midnight]):*

	WED	THU	FRI	SAT	SUN	MON
(Night time)	6:00 **PM:** *(Jesus eats Last Supper)* 10:00 **PM:** *(Garden)* 12:00 **AM:** *(Interrog'n)* 5:00 **AM:** *(to Pilate)* 5:59 **AM**	6:00 **PM:** *(Jewish Passover)* ***(First 'night' in the grave)*** 5:59 **AM**	6:00 **PM** ***(Second 'night' in the grave)*** 5:59 **AM**	6:00 **PM** ***(Third 'night' in the grave)*** 5:59 **AM**	6:00 **PM:** *(End of his '3 days & 3 nights' in grave: Resurrect'n)* 5:59 **AM**	6:00 **PM** *(Appears, at Emmaus)* *(Appears, with the apostles)* *(Plants Seed of Holy Ghost)* 5:59 **AM**
(Daylight)	6:00 **AM:** *(Interrog'n & Torture Ends)* 9:00 **AM:** *(CRUCIFIED)* 3:00 **PM** *(DIED)* 5:00 **PM** *(BURIED)*	6:00 **AM** ***(First 'day' in the grave)*** 5:59 **PM**	6:00 **AM** ***(Second 'day' in the grave)*** 5:59 **PM**	6:00 **AM** ***(Third 'day' in the grave)*** 5:59 **PM**	6:00 **AM:** *(Tomb is found empty)* *(Jesus appears to the Women)* 5:59 **PM**	6:00 **AM** 5:59 **PM**
	Preparation Day	*Feast of the Passover*			*Resurrection Day*	

Now, when Mary (the Magdalene) and Mary (the mother of Jesus) had left from the Lord's burial *(just before 6:00 p.m., as Wednesday became Thursday)*, they were not allowed to return again (to visit the dead) until Sunday *(after both the Annual Sabbath and the Weekly Sabbath had passed) – (See; Fig. 2 [pg. 261])*. Therefore; early on Sunday morning (the first day of the week) the women returned again, to the tomb *(Mary [the Magdalene]...Mary [mother of Jesus]...and Salome* [mother of James and John]). And they brought with them sweet spices and ointments they had prepared for Jesus' proper burial. As the women walked along the path to the graveyard that morning, they began to question among themselves who would roll away the great stone, for them (so that they could get into the tomb to anoint the Lord's body). — *(Matt 28:1 & Mark 16:1-3 & Luke 23:56—24:1 & John 20:1)*

No sooner had the question arose among the women, than did the earth begin to quake violently at their feet. For, an angel of the Lord had descended from heaven at that very moment, and rolled back the stone from the opening of the tomb — and sat down upon the stone, to wait for the women to arrive. And his countenance was like lightning, and his raiment was white as snow. And for fear of him, the Roman soldiers who guarded the Tomb, shook — and then fainted dead away. Now, when the women finally arrived at the tomb, they found the great stone rolled away, already. And when they entered the tomb *(to anoint the Lord's body)*, they found the tomb empty — *(See; Fig. 2 [pg. 261])*. The women were paralyzed with confusion and grief (believing someone had stolen the Lord's body), when they suddenly noticed the angel standing on the right side of the tomb — dressed in a long, white garment. The angel said to them; "Fear not. You have come seeking Jesus, who was crucified. He is risen; as he said. Come and examine the place where he was laid." Then he told them; "Go, and tell his disciples that he is risen from the dead — and that he goes before you, into Galilee. There, you shall see him; as he told you." — *(Matt 28:2-7 & Mark 16:4-7 & Luke 24:2-3)*

With that; the women fled the tomb (to return to the disciples). And they spoke to no man, along the way — for they trembled with fear and amazement. But, Mary *(the Magdalene)* ran directly to Peter and the 'disciple whom Jesus loved' *(presumably; her brother, Lazarus)*. And she sobbed as she told them that someone had taken Jesus' body away, and she didn't know where they had laid him. So, Peter and the 'disciple whom Jesus loved' ran, together, to the tomb. And the 'disciple whom Jesus loved' *(being younger)* outran Peter *(who was older)*; arriving first, at the tomb. And stooping down, to look inside, he saw the linen clothes lying there *(yet, he had no desire to go*

inside the tomb). Then came Peter, from behind, and
entered into the tomb — and saw the grave clothes. And
he saw the napkin which had been around Jesus head,
not lying with the other clothing; but folded up in a
place by itself. Then did the 'disciple whom Jesus
loved' go inside the tomb. And when he saw with his
own eyes that Jesus was gone, he believed Mary was
right; that someone had taken the Lord's body away. —
(Matt 28:8 & Mark 16:8 & John 20:2-9)

Then, the disciples left the tomb and returned to
their home, leaving the women to linger around the
tomb, greatly perplexed. And as Mary stood there,
weeping, she stooped down to look into the tomb again
— and she saw two angels wearing white garments,
sitting inside. One angel was sitting at the head —
and the other, at the feet — where the body of Jesus
had lain. And when the women saw the angels, they
bowed down their faces to the earth, in fear. But the
angels said; "Why do you still seek the living among
the dead? He is not here, but is risen. Remember that
he told you (when he was with you in Galilee) he must
be crucified, and then be raised from the grave three

days later?" And immediately Jesus' Words were brought to their remembrance. — *(Luke 24:4-8 & John 20:10-12)*

And when the angels asked Mary; "Why do you weep," she answered them; "Because they have taken away my Lord, and I do not know where they have laid him." And as she turned quickly to run to the disciples; there, in her path, appeared the risen Jesus — *(See; Fig. 2 [pg. 261])*. Jesus said to Mary; "Woman, why do you weep? Whom do you seek?" And (mistaking him, at first, for the gardener) she said; "Sir, if you have taken him somewhere; tell me where you have laid him and I will take him away." But Jesus said to her; "Mary..." And the moment he called her name, Mary knew him. She called out; "Master!" And all the women fell upon Jesus' feet, and held fast; worshipping him. But, Jesus told them; "Do not touch me yet; for I am not yet ascended to my Father. *(For me, this passage is proof enough that Jesus did not ascend into Paradise four days earlier, when he died.)*" He instructed them; "Go and tell my brethren, 'I must ascend to my Father and your Father; and to my God and your God'. Tell them to go into Galilee — and there, they shall see me." *(They would later meet, in*

Galilee, and accompany Jesus back to Mt. Olivet, where he would finally ascend.) **- (Matt 28:9-10 & Mark 16:9 & John 20:13-17)**

And when the women departed, to deliver the Lord's message to the disciples, some of the Roman soldiers *(who had fainted at the tomb)* returned, instead, to the Jews; telling the Chief Priests everything that had happened at the tomb. And after coming to an agreement, the Jews gave the Roman soldiers a large payment — instructing them; "Say that his disciples came by night, and stole him away while we slept. And if it be reported to Pilate, we will back up your story." So, the Roman soldiers took the money, and did as they were taught. Meanwhile; Mary *(the Magdalene)*, Joanna, Mary (the mother of Jesus and James) — and the other women that were with them, had returned to report all these things to the eleven remaining apostles (and the rest of the assembly of disciples). But when the women told the assembly about Jesus' resurrection and appearance to them, their words seemed like idle tales — and the assembly didn't believe that Jesus had risen. But Peter stood up and ran back to the tomb. And stooping down, he looked once again upon the linen clothes laying there all by themselves. And he departed again; wondering, in himself. — *(Matt 28:11-15 & Mark 16:10-11 & Luke 24:9-12 & John 20:18)*

Later that afternoon; two of Jesus' disciples walked along together, down the road to Emmaus *(which is about 7 miles away from Jerusalem)*. And as Cleopas and Simon walked along — talking about all the heartbreaking events that had taken place in Jerusalem throughout the week — it came to pass that the risen Jesus himself drew near to them, and began to walk with them — *(See; Fig. 2 [pg. 261])*. But they didn't recognize him, either (and this Simon was not Simon Peter). And Jesus said to his two disciples; "What is this that you speak of, as you walk — which makes you so sad?" And Cleopas answered him; "Are you a stranger in Jerusalem? Have you not seen and heard all that has come to pass there, in these days?" And Jesus asked; "What things?" And they recounted to him how the rulers of Israel had taken and crucified their beloved Lord; whom they had trusted to be the Messiah. And how — that very morning — the women of their group had discovered his body missing from the grave; claiming that he had appeared to them, moments later, in the flesh. And that certain of their men had raced to the tomb to see if it were true, and found it exactly as the women had said. And finally, Jesus said to them; "How slow of heart to believe all that the prophets have spoken. Ought not Christ to have suffered these things and to enter into his glory *(according to prophecy)*? And starting with Moses — and throughout all the prophets, thereafter — Christ expounded to them in all the scriptures everything concerning himself." *(In other words; 'Why are you pining about all this as if it were a bad thing?')* — **(Mark 16:12 & Luke 24:13-27)**

And as they were drawing near to the village, Jesus acted as though he would have passed right by it. But Cleopas and Simon said; "You may as well come into this village with us; for, evening is approaching." And so, Jesus went in to Emmaus to dine with them. And as they sat down to dinner, Jesus took bread, and blessed and brake it — and he gave it to the two disciples. Immediately, their eyes were opened and they 'knew' him (and immediately, the risen Jesus vanished from their sight). And they looked at each other, and said; "Didn't our hearts burn within us while he talked with us by the way — and when he spoke to us of the scriptures?" And they rose up that same hour and returned to Jerusalem to find the eleven remaining apostles (and the rest of the assembly of disciples) gathered together, in the house — *(See; Fig. 2 [pg. 261])*. Upon entering the house, they exclaimed; "The Lord is risen, indeed! He hath appeared to us!" And they told the whole story of how Jesus' appeared to them on the road to Emmaus — and how he was made known to them in the breaking of bread. But the assembly didn't believe the testimony of these two men, either. *(So far, 'word of mouth' simply wasn't enough to make someone else 'believe'.)*

— *(Mark 16:13 & Luke 24:28-35)*

(And for reasons undisclosed by scripture, Thomas apparently rose up and left the house, at this point. This, we know; because when the risen Jesus, himself, appears in the midst of them — just moments later — Thomas is said to have been missing from among the eleven [John 20:24].) And so; with the doors still closed upon them (for fear of the Jews), Jesus suddenly appeared in the room — *(See; Fig. 2 [pg.*

261]). He said to them; "Peace be to you." And the
assembly was terrified; supposing him to be some
spirit. But Jesus immediately showed them his hands
and his side. And while they were yet afraid to
believe that it were true, he asked them; "Have you
any meat?" And they gave him broiled fish and an
honeycomb — and he ate it, before them. *(Jesus had
told the disciples [in Luke 22:16] that he would not
eat again until all is fulfilled in the Kingdom of God
— and he had said [dying, on the cross], 'It is
finished'. It was Jesus' willing death that sealed the
salvation of the Kingdom of God — and there is no
salvation, apart from his blood covering us.)* And
Jesus told them; "These are the Words I spoke to you
while I was yet with you; that all things written in
the Law and in the prophets and in the Psalms *(in the
Old Testament)* concerning me *(Christ)*, must be
fulfilled *(in other words; 'I must die and be raised
again, to save you')*." Then, did all the disciples
rejoice (the Lord, himself, having brought the truth
of his Words back to their remembrance). Then he told
them, again; "Peace be to you. As my Father has sent
me, even so I send you *(asking you to sacrifice your*

worldly life in order to save those who are lost)."
And when he had said this; he breathed on them, and
said; "Receive the Holy Ghost *(planting inside of them
the Seed of the Holy Spirit of Truth [however, that
'Seed' would not become fully sanctified until
Pentecost]) — (See; Fig. 2 [pg. 261]).*" For now; he
anointed them, saying; "Whose soever sins you leave
upon them, they will remain unforgiven — and whose
soever sins you bear and forgive, they will be
forgiven *(remit -vs.- retain; also see John 10:33-36 &
Matt 16:18-19)."* *(Having made these men 'children of
God' by planting the Seed of the Holy Spirit inside of
them, Jesus was letting them know they now have the
power [within themselves] to forgive sins [and,
thereby; to save souls]. Likewise; they have the power
to condemn souls.)* But Thomas was not present among
them during this particular appearance of Jesus. And
when Thomas was reunited with the disciples, later,
the disciples tried to tell him that the risen Jesus
had appeared to them — but Thomas doubted every word
they said. He told them; "Unless I see the holes in
his hands and put my finger into the holes, and thrust
my hand into his side, I will not believe." *(Thomas*

went down in history as 'the one who wouldn't believe' — but, in truth; none of them were able to believe until Jesus made himself known to them.) **- (Luke 24:36-44 & John 20:19-25)**

After that day, Jesus appeared to the eleven apostles again (eight days later) when they were assembled together in the house with the doors closed upon them *(still fearing the Jews)*. Appearing, he said to them; "Peace be to you." And to Thomas, he said; "Reach out your finger and touch my hands. And reach out your hand and thrust it into my side — and be not faithless, but believing." And Thomas — seeing the holes in his Master's body — answered; "My Lord and my God." And Jesus told him; "Thomas, because you have seen me, you have believed. Blessed are they that have not seen, and yet, have believed." *(I confess I don't know who Jesus is referring to, in this verse. Everyone mentioned in the scriptures up to this point is said to have 'not' believed until Jesus made himself 'known' to them.)* And Jesus did many other signs and wonders that are not written in this book, so that we might believe that Jesus is the risen Christ, the Son of God — and that believing, we might have life, through his name. — *(Mark 16:14 & John 20:26-31)*

Then went the eleven apostles into Galilee; to the very mountain where Jesus had told them to meet him. And Jesus showed himself again to them, at the Sea of Tiberius; and it was on this wise: There were gathered together Peter, Thomas, Nathanael — and the brothers, James and John — and two unnamed disciples *(the 'disciple whom Jesus loved', being among them).* Now, (Simon) Peter decided to go fishing while they waited for the Lord — and the others also went with him. And they entered into their ship. And fishing all night, they caught nothing. But when morning was come; suddenly, Jesus appeared on the shore and called out to them; "Children, have you any meat?" And they said; "No." And Jesus told them; "Cast your net on the right hand side of the ship and you will find fish." Now, they did not know that it was Jesus who spoke to them. Nevertheless; they cast in their nets, as was suggested — and immediately, they could not draw the net back in (for the multitude of fish that were caught). — *(Matt 28:16 & John 21:1-7)*

And because of the sheer bounty of fish provided, the 'disciple whom Jesus loved' said to Peter; "It is the Lord." And when Peter heard that it was the Lord, he put on his fisher's coat (for he was naked) and he cast himself into the sea. And some other disciples came in a little ship, to help Peter drag in their nets. Now, as soon as they were come to land, they saw a fire of coals (prepared, of Jesus), and fish laid thereon, and bread. And Jesus told them; "Bring some of the fish that you have caught, and come and dine with me." And no one asked Jesus, 'Who are you?' because they all knew who he was. Then Jesus took bread and gave to the disciples — and the fish, likewise. And this was now the third time that Jesus showed himself to the assembly of apostles and disciples after being raised from the dead *(and he had still not yet ascended into Paradise)*. — *(John 21:6-14)*

After they had dined, Jesus said to Simon (Peter); "Simon, son of Jonas; do you love me?" And he answered; "Yes Lord; you know that I love you." And Jesus said; "Feed my lambs." A few moments later, Jesus said to him a second time; "Simon, son of Jonas;

do you love me?" And again he answered; "Yes Lord; you know that I love you." And Jesus said; "Feed my sheep." And again a third time, Jesus asked him; "Simon, son of Jonas; do you love me?" And Simon Peter was grieved because Jesus kept asking him. And he said to him; "Lord, you know all things; you know that I love you." And Jesus said; "Feed my sheep." *(Some people believe that Jesus asked this question of Simon [Peter] three times because Peter had verbally 'denied' Jesus three times — and Jesus wanted Peter to grasp the connection between his 'forgiveness' and the critical 'job' that he was being redeemed to perform.)* Then Jesus told Peter; "Of a truth, I say to you that when you were young, you dressed yourself and walked wherever you wanted to go. But when you are old, you will stretch out your hands and someone else will dress you — and take you where you would rather not go." (Jesus was signifying by what death Peter would glorify God.) And Jesus told him; "Follow me (anyway)." **— *(John 21:15-19)***

And then Peter turned around to look at the 'Disciple whom Jesus loved' — and he asked Jesus; "And what shall this man do *(for the Kingdom)*?" *(This was,* presumably, Lazarus — who, had already been resurrected from death. We already know that he was charged with taking care of Jesus' mother, Mary, for the rest of her life.) But Jesus told him; "If I want him to remain here until I return (at the Second Coming), what is that to you? You just need to follow me (on the path of self-sacrifice; for the Kingdom)." Then it was spread abroad that the 'disciple whom Jesus loved' would never die — but that isn't what Jesus actually said — he just said, 'what business would it be' of Peter's. It is stated, in these passages, that it was this very disciple (the 'disciple whom Jesus loved') which testified of all these things (writing them in the New Testament book we call the 'Gospel of John'); and we know that his testimony is true. And when the disciples saw Jesus, they worshipped him — but some, doubted. (Some theologians speculate that the 'disciple whom Jesus loved' was, in fact, Mary [the Magdalene]. But Peter confirms, in the above passages, that the disciple in question was, in fact, a man — and therefore; it could not have been Mary.) — **(Matt 28:17 & John 21:20-24)**

And the risen Jesus opened their understanding so that they could understand the scriptures. And he told them; "All power is given to me, in heaven and in earth. Thus it is written and thus it behooved Christ to suffer and to rise from the dead the third day — and that repentance *(committing our earthly life to serve God instead of ourselves)* and remission of sins *(forgiveness)* should be preached in my name, among all nations — beginning at Jerusalem. Go, therefore, into all the world; preach the Gospel to every creature in all nations, baptizing in the name of the Father and of the Son and of the Holy Ghost. He that believes and is baptized *(reborn as a child of God; receiving the Seed of the Holy Spirit of Truth and becoming fully sanctified)* shall be saved. But, he that does not believe, shall remain damned *(condemned, under sin)*." And he said; "And these signs shall follow those who believe *(and are reborn; a child of God)*: In my name *('Savior')*, they will cast out devils. They shall speak with a new tongue *(as a new man)*. They shall take up serpents *(evil spirits)*. They shall not be hurt by drinking any deadly thing *(I believe this refers to us having the ability to cast out any unclean spirit we may inadvertently drink in).* They shall lay hands on the sick, and they will recover. Teach the nations to do as I have commanded you. You are Witnesses of all these things — and I will send the 'promise' of my Father upon you *(which is the full sanctification of our Seed [of the Holy Spirit])*." *(Now, the disciples had become able to receive specific anointings from the Holy Spirit from the moment they were 'water-baptized' (in the name of the Father [having repented, and submitted their fleshen souls for cleansing and service to God]). And some time later, they were also 'blood-baptized' (in the name of the Son [receiving the Seed of the Holy Spirit of Truth into their heart; planted there, by the risen Jesus when he first appeared to them behind closed doors, saying, 'receive the Holy Ghost'].)* In the current passages; Jesus is now instructing the disciples to go and wait in the city of Jerusalem to be 'spirit-baptized' *(in the name of the Holy Ghost [receiving the full anointing of power from on high; becoming fully empowered/sanctified children of God]).* Jesus said to them; "John *(the Baptist)* truly baptized you with water *(unto repentance)* — but you must also be (fire) baptized *(fully anointed)* of the Holy Ghost, not many days from now *(at Pentecost)*." He said; "You shall receive power after the Holy Ghost is come upon you *(fully anointing/sanctifying you)* — and you shall be Witnesses for me from Jerusalem unto the uttermost part of the earth." And Jesus promised his disciples; "I will be with you always; until the end of the world." *(And, in all; the risen Jesus will appear to his disciples for a total of 40 days [after his resurrection] — before finally ascending into Paradise, to be with God.)* **- (Matt 28:18-20 & Mark 16:15-18 & Luke 24:45-49 & Acts 1:3-8)**

Then, Jesus led his disciples back from Galilee; bringing them as far as to Bethany, in Mount Olivet. There; Jesus lifted up his hands and blessed them. And as he stood blessing them, he was carried away into heaven and swallowed up in a cloud *(to take his place at the right hand of God; ascending into Paradise)*. And as the disciples beheld his ascension into heaven, two men stood by them, in white apparel — who said; "You men of Galilee; why do you stand gazing up into heaven? He will return to you in like manner as you have watched him leave." And the disciples worshipped their Lord and joyfully returned to Jerusalem to await the promise of God *(the full baptism of the Holy Ghost). (It is very interesting to note the sequence and timing of the sanctification events of the disciples/apostles: They first needed to bring their minds and wills to repentance and willingness to serve only God's will [so that the Seed of God could be received into a 'cleansed'/prepared vessel]. Next; they needed to invite the Seed of God into their heart [so that the power of the Holy Spirit could be poured into that Seed, to inflate their heart].) − (Mark 16:19 & Luke 24:50-52 & Acts 1:9-12)*

And when the disciples entered back into the house, they all went up into the large upper room where the eleven abode. These all continued with one heart and mind, in prayer and supplication, with the women and Mary (the mother of Jesus) and Jesus' brethren; awaiting the promise of God. And in those days, Peter stood up in the midst of about one-hundred-twenty disciples, and said; "Men and brethren; this scripture had to be fulfilled; which the Holy Ghost − by the mouth of David − spoke before, concerning Judas (who betrayed Jesus). For he was numbered with us and had obtained part of this ministry — but, is now lost to us. Now; out of these men which have companied with us all the time that the Lord Jesus walked with us, one must be chosen [and ordained] to be a witness with us of the Lord's resurrection." And so, they appointed two candidates—Joseph and Matthias. And they prayed for God to show them which of these two disciples He wanted to take part of their ministry and apostleship. And when they had prayed, they cast forth their lots and the lot fell upon Matthias — and so, he was numbered among the apostles. — *(Acts 1:13-26)*

Now, Pentecost was an annual celebration observed fifty days after the day of the Passover Feast. In this particular year, that happened to be fifty days after Jesus *(our 'Passover Lamb')* was buried. And on this fiftieth day, the disciples were still gathered together in the upper room of the house (waiting to receive the promise of God) when, suddenly; there came a sound from heaven as of a rushing, mighty wind. And the sound filled the whole house. And there appeared, over the head of every soul, as it were a cloven tongue of fire — and it sat upon each one as they were filled with the power of the Holy Ghost; one hundred twenty souls, in all *(per Acts 2:15)*. And they began to speak in the tongues other lands, as the spirit gave them utterance. And there were many devout Jewish men in Jerusalem, at that time — from every nation (and language) under heaven. And when news of what was transpiring at the house spread throughout the city, many of these devout Jewish men were drawn to the house to witness it for themselves. And as they listened to the disciples speaking in a variety of foreign languages, some of these devout Jews said; "These disciples are all Galileans. How is it that each of us hears them speaking in our own native language?" *(The 'lost sheep' of Israel had long ago been scattered throughout the earth, into various lands and languages [Parthia, Mede, Elam, Mesopotamia, Judea, Cappadocia, Pontus, Asia, Phrygia, Pamphlia, Egypt, Cyrene, Rome, Crete and Arabia]. But, now — at a time when God needed for everyone in the world to hear the message of His wonderful works — everyone spoke different languages. Therefore, God gifted each disciple with a particular foreign tongue, so that they could go and tell his Word to the whole world.*

The gift of tongues was a critical first gift to

receive, in those early days of Christian ministry.) —

(Acts 2:1-11)

And the crowds were all amazed — but some were in

doubt; wondering what all this meant. There were also

some in the audience who mocked them; accusing the

disciples of being drunk. Therefore, Peter lifted up

his voice and said; "You men of Judea — and all of you

who dwell in Jerusalem — listen to me: These men are

not drunk (seeing that it is only 9:00 o'clock in the

morning). What you are witnessing, is the prophecy

which was foretold to us by the Prophet Joel — which

said, 'And it shall come to pass in the last days that

I will pour out my spirit *(the Holy Spirit of Truth;*

the 'voice' of God) upon all flesh, and your sons and

daughters shall prophecy *(proclaim the Word of God)*.

And your young men shall see visions and your old men

shall dream dreams. And on my servants and on my

handmaidens I will pour out, in those days, of my

(Holy) Spirit — and they shall prophesy. And I will

show wonders in heaven and earth; blood, fire and

vapor of smoke. The sun shall be darkened and the moon

shall be turned into blood — all, before that great

and notable day of the Lord *(the Second Coming)* come.
And whoever shall call upon the name of the Lord shall
be saved'." – *(Acts 2:12-21)*

Then, did Peter deliver God's message to the lost
sheep of Israel — saying; "You men of Israel, hear
these Words: Jesus of Nazareth — a man approved of God
before you by the miracles that God did through him.
in your midst (as you well know); he — being delivered
by our rulers (and the foreknowledge of God)—Israel
has crucified and killed. And God (three days later)
raised him up from the dead — having loosed the pains
of death, because it was not possible that he should
be holden of it; for, David prophesied that God would
not leave his soul in hell (the grave) — and of this
(resurrection) we are all witnesses. Therefore; being
exalted by the right hand of God, and having received
the promise of the Holy Ghost *(which is the full
baptism of the Holy Ghost)* — Jesus has shed forth
this, which you now see and hear *(the voice/Words of
the Holy Spirit being proclaimed through the
disciples)*. Therefore; let all the house of Israel
know, assuredly, that God has made that same Jesus —

whom you have crucified — both Lord and Christ." — *(Acts 2:22-36)*

Now, when the lost sheep (in the crowd) heard these Words, they were pricked in their heart — and they said to Peter and the other apostles; "Brethren, what shall we do?" And Peter said to them; "Repent and be baptized — every one of you — in the name of Jesus Christ; for the remission of sins. And you will receive the Holy Ghost (baptism). For, the promise (of full sanctification) is to you and to your children — and all those who are afar off (in time); even as many as the Lord our God shall call to himself." Then, they that gladly received his Word were baptized. And about three thousand of the lost sheep of Israel were saved, that day. And they continued, steadfastly, in the apostles' doctrine, and fellowship, and communion, and in prayers. And they were continually in the Temple (praising and blessing God). And they went forth into the world, preaching everywhere — the Lord working through them and with them, and confirming the Word with signs *(miracles/increase)* that followed — and having favor with all the people. And there are so many other things which Jesus did, that; if all of it were written, we suppose the world itself could not contain the books that should be written. *(This passage clearly describes a quantity of Holy Scripture [presented by Jesus] far exceeding the volume that could possibly be contained in just one book. For this reason, alone, we should never lightly disregard any book that presents itself to be inspired by God and encourages us to worship God and His son [particularly, any Word that claims to have originated from the very mouth of Jesus, himself] simply because that book is not currently 'bound' into a present-day Bible.)* And the Lord added to the church, daily, such as should be saved. Amen. **– (Mark 16:20 & Luke 24:53 & John 21:25 & Acts 2:37-47)**

(This has been the story of Jesus Christ) — in whom we have redemption through his blood (the forgiveness of sins); he, who is the image of the invisible God and the firstborn of every creature. For by him were all things created that are in heaven, and that are in earth — visible and invisible. Thrones, dominions, principalities or powers — all things were created by him and for him. And he existed before all things — and by him, all things consist. And he who is

the beginning and the first reborn from the dead, is the head of the body *(the church)*; so that in all things he might have the preeminence. For it pleased the Father that in Christ Jesus should all fullness *(of Holy Spirit)* dwell. And he, himself, has made peace through the blood of his cross; to reconcile all things unto himself — whether they be things in earth, or things in heaven. And you, that were sometime alienated and enemies in your mind, by wicked works; yet he has reconciled all things in the body of his flesh (through death) to present you holy and blameless and unreproveable in His sight (if ye continue in the faith, grounded and settled, and be not moved away from the hope of the gospel which ye have heard and which was preached to every creature which is under heaven). — *(Colossians 1:14-23)*

END

APPENDIX A – GOSPEL GRID KEY

HARMONY of the GOSPELS

EVENT / ACTIVITY		MATH	MARK	LUKE	JOHN	ACTS
MARY becomes pregnant	Pg. 7--8			1:5-33	1:1-18	
	Pg. 8--9			1:34-38		
MARY visits Elisabeth	Pg. 9			1:39-56		
JOHN the Baptist is born	Pg. 9--10			1:57-80 *(& 1:5-25)		
Pregnant MARY returns home	Pg. 10--11	1:18-24				
JESUS is born	Pg. 11--12	1:25		2:1-7		
Birth of MESSIAH announced	Pg. 12--13			2:8-14		
	Pg. 13			2:15-20		
WISE MEN see the star	Pg. 13--14	2:1-2				
JESUS is 1-month-old	Pg. 14--15			2:21-38		
WISE MEN in Jerusalem	Pg. 15--16	2:3-8				
WISE MEN in Bethlehem	Pg. 16--17	2:9-12				

HARMONY of the GOSPELS

EVENT / ACTIVITY		MATH	MARK	LUKE	JOHN	ACTS
Holy family flees to Egypt	Pg. 17	2:13-15				
HEROD kills all baby boys	Pg. 17	2:16-18				
Holy family returns; to Nazareth	Pg. 18	2:19-23		2:39-40		
JESUS is 12-years-old	Pg. 18--19			2:40-52		
THE BEGINNING OF 'THE MINISTRY OF JESUS CHRIST':						
JOHN the Baptist is 'activated'	Pg. 19--20	3:1-4	1:1-3	3:1-6		
WHY JOHN baptizes [with water]	Pg. 20--21	3:5-12	1:4-8	3:7-18		
	Pg. 22			*(1:13-17)	1:6-9	
JESUS is water-baptized by JOHN	Pg. 22--24	3:13-17	1:9-11	3:21-23	1:14-15	
JESUS tempted in the wilderness	Pg. 24--25	4:1-11	1:12-13	4:1-13		
SIMON [PETER] follows JESUS... (brining ANDREW along)	Pg. 25--26				1:19-42	
JESUS BEGINS HIS MINISTRY; HEADING OUT INTO GALILEE:						
JESUS 'calls' PHILIP... (who, brings NATHANIEL along)	Pg. 27				1:43-51	

Appendix A -- (Pg. 2 of 22)

HARMONY of the GOSPELS

EVENT / ACTIVITY		MATH	MARK	LUKE	JOHN	ACTS
JESUS' family joins his ministry, in CANA, and they move on to CAPERNAUM-(homebase)	Pg.27--28	* (Jesus' 1st MIRACLE happens here)			2:1-12	
BEGINNING OF 2nd YEAR of JESUS MINISTRY; PASSOVER WEEK:						
First PASSOVER of JESUS ministry; in JERUSALEM, at end of 1st year of ministry; overturns merchants tables in Temple	Pg.28--29				2:13-25	
NICODEMUS questions JESUS	Pg.29--30				3:1-21	
JOHN & JESUS baptize in JUDEA; (JOHN not in prison, yet)	Pg.30--31				3:22-36	
JOHN imprisoned. JESUS moved [by spirit] to return to GALILEE; meets SAMARITAN WOMAN	Pg.31--33	4:12	1:14-15	4:14	4:1-27	
	Pg.33--34				4:28-43	
JESUS returns to CANA of GALILEE; heals the NOBELMAN'S SON	Pg.34	* (Jesus' 2nd MIRACLE happens here)			4:43-54	
JESUS is cast out of NAZARETH	Pg.35--36	4:13-17		4:15-30		

Appendix A -- (Pg. 3 of 22)

HARMONY of the GOSPELS

EVENT / ACTIVITY		MATH	MARK	LUKE	JOHN	ACTS
JESUS 'calls' SIMON (PETER), ANDREW, JAMES & JOHN	Pg. 36--37	4:18-22	1:14-20	*5:1-11		
JESUS returns to CAPERNAUM; casts out an unclean spirit	Pg. 37--38		1:21-28	4:31-37		
JESUS heals SIMON's mom-in-law	Pg. 38	8:14-17	1:29-39	4:37-44		
JESUS heals a LEPER	Pg. 38--39	*8:1-4	1:40-45	5:12-16		
JESUS heals man LOWERED through roof	Pg. 39--40	9:1-8	2:1-12	5:17-26		
JESUS 'calls' MATTHEW & LEVI-(JAMES; son of ALPHAEUS)	Pg. 40--41	9:9-13	2:13-17	5:27-32		
Why don't JESUS' disciples 'fast'?	Pg. 41	9:14-17	2:18-22	5:33-39		
JESUS returns to JERUSALEM; heals a crippled man at the POOL	Pg. 42--43				5:1-18	
JESUS testifies of himself	Pg. 43				5:19-24	
	Pg. 43--45				5:25-36	
	Pg. 45--46				5:37-47	

Appendix A -- (Pg. 4 of 22)

HARMONY of the GOSPELS

EVENT / ACTIVITY		MATH	MARK	LUKE	JOHN	ACTS
JESUS plucks CORN on the Sabbath day	Pg. 46--47	12:1-8	2:23-28	6:1-5		
JESUS heals WITHERED HAND in Temple	Pg. 47	12:9-14	3:1-6	6:6-11		
JESUS returns to GALILEE; he ORDAINS the TWELVE 'APOSTLES' to grow in JESUS' 'word'	Pg. 49--50	12:15-21 *(& 5:1-2)	3:7-19	6:12-19		
JESUS gives SERMON on the MOUNT	Pg. 50--51	*5:3-12		6:20-26		
God's children are the 'Salt of the Earth'	Pg. 51--52	5:13-20				
Live, a BETTER way	Pg. 52--53	5:21-22				
	53	5:23-32				
	Pg. 54	5:33-6:4		6:27-36		
	Pg. 55	6:5-7:5		*6:39-42		
	Pg. 56	7:6-27		*6:37-38		
How to tell 'born-agains' from 'worldly'	Pg. 57	7:28-8:1		6:43-49		
JESUS returns to CAPERNAUM; heals CENTURION'S SERVANT	Pg. 58	8:5-13		7:1-10		

Appendix A -- (Pg. 5 of 22)

HARMONY of the GOSPELS

EVENT / ACTIVITY		MATH	MARK	LUKE	JOHN	ACTS
JESUS RESURRECTS the WIDOW'S SON	Pg. 58--59			7:11-17		
JOHN/Baptist questions JESUS from prison [in GALILEE]	Pg. 59--60	11:2-6		7:18-23		
JESUS explains JOHN'S importance	Pg. 60--61	11:7-19		7:24-35		
	Pg. 61--62	11:20-30				
MARY anoints JESUS feet with oil; at the home of SIMON the Pharisee...	Pg. 62--64			7:36-50		
JESUS casts SEVEN DEVILS out of her	Pg. 64--65			8:1-3		
PHARISEES BLASPHEME the Holy Spirit	Pg. 65--66	12:22-37	3:20-30			
	Pg. 66--67	12:38-50	3:31-35			
PARABLES from the boat, in GALILEE; the SOWER planting on different soils...	Pg. 67--68	13:1-17	4:1-13	8:4-10		
the TARES & WHEAT grow together...	Pg. 68--70	13:18-23	4:14-29	8:11-18		
the MUSTARDSEED grows into a tree...; the LEAVEN put into batch of dough...	Pg. 70--71	13:24-35	4:30-34	8:19-21		

HARMONY of the GOSPELS

EVENT / ACTIVITY		MATH	MARK	LUKE	JOHN	ACTS
the TREASURE hidden in the field... the PEARL of great value... the NET casted into the sea	Pg. 71--72	13:36-53				
WINDSTORM on the SEA...'Peace, be still':	Pg. 72--73	*8:18-27	4:35-41	8:22-25		
2 possessed men from the tombs; devils enter heard of SWINE	Pg. 73	8:28-34	5:1-20	8:26-39		
DISEASED WOMAN touches JESUS clothes	Pg. 74--75	9:18-22	5:21-34	8:40-48		
JESUS RESURRECTS JAIRUS' DAUGHTER	Pg. 75	9:23-26	5:35-43	8:49-56		
JESUS heals TWO BLIND MEN	Pg. 75--76	9:27-34				
JESUS returns to NAZARETH... they still have no faith	Pg. 76	*13:54-58	6:1-6			
	Pg. 77	9:35-38				
JESUS ANOINTS the TWELVE APOSTLES AGAIN. This time; to send them out to cast out devils, heal and resurrect	Pg. 77--79	10:1-14	6:7-11	9:1-5		
	Pg. 79-80	10:15-11:1	6:12-13	9:6		

HARMONY of the GOSPELS

EVENT / ACTIVITY		MATH	MARK	LUKE	JOHN	ACTS
JOHN/Baptist is BEHEADED in prison; his disciples now become JESUS' disciples	Pg. 80--81	14:1-13	6:14-33	9:7-10	6:2-3	
BEGINNING OF 3rd YEAR of JESUS MINISTRY; PASSOVER WEEK:						
JESUS feeds 5,000 with LOAVES & FISHES; 2nd PASSOVER of JESUS' ministry	Pg. 81--82	14:14-21	6:34-44	9:11-17	6:4-13	
JESUS WALKS ON WATER during storm	Pg. 82--83	14:22-36	6:45-56		6:14-21	
JESUS returns to CAPERNAUM; teaching	Pg. 83--84				6:22-34	
	Pg. 85				6:35-40	
	Pg. 85--86				6:41-51	
Many disciples WALK AWAY from JESUS	Pg. 86--88				6:52-71	
	Pg. 88--89	15:1-20	7:1-23		7:1	
JESUS goes to TYRE and SIDON; 'crumbs from the children's table'	Pg. 89--90	15:21-28	7:24-30			
JESUS returns to GALILEE; FEEDS 4,000 with LOAVES & FISHES	Pg. 90--91	15:29-38	7:31-8:9			
JESUS goes to DALMANUTHA (MAGDALA)	Pg. 91--92	15:39-16:12	8:10-21			

Appendix A -- (Pg. 8 of 22)

HARMONY of the GOSPELS

EVENT / ACTIVITY		MATH	MARK	LUKE	JOHN	ACTS
JESUS goes to BETHSAIDA & CAESAREA PHILIPPI	Pg. 92--93	16:13-20	8:22-30	9:18-21		
JESUS begins to prepare his disciples for his crucifixion. PETER rebukes him	Pg. 93--95	16:21-28	8:31-9:1	9:22-27		
JESUS' TRANSFIGURATION on mountain at Sea of GALILEE	Pg. 95	17:1-8	9:2-8	9:28-36		
	Pg. 95--96	17:9-13	9:9-13			
The disciples COULDN'T CAST OUT a devil	Pg. 96--99	17:14-21	9:14-29	9:37-43		
JESUS returns to CAPERNAUM: PETER gives a tax collector a coin from a fish' mouth.	Pg. 99--100	17:22-27	9:30-32	9:43-45	7:2-9	
JESUS returns to CAPERNAUM: teaching	Pg. 100--101	18:1-5	9:33-37	9:46-48		
	Pg. 101--103	18:6-14	9:38-50	9:49-50		
	Pg. 103--104	18:15-22				
PARABLES at the house, in CAPERNAUM: the WICKED SERVANT; not forgiving the debt of fellow servans	Pg. 104--105	18:23-35				

Appendix A -- (Pg. 9 of 22)

HARMONY of the GOSPELS

EVENT / ACTIVITY		MATH	MARK	LUKE	JOHN	ACTS
JESUS passes through SAMARIA	Pg. 107--109	*8:19-22		9:51-62		
JESUS returns to JERUSALEM, to teach	Pg. 109--110				7:10-20	
JESUS departs, to MOUNT of OLIVES	Pg. 110--111				7:21-31	
	Pg. 112				7:32-8:1	
WOMAN CAUGHT in ADULTERY	Pg. 112--113				8:2-11	
JESUS continues teaching, in JERUSALEM	Pg. 113--115				8:12-30	
JESUS exposes the 'children of the devil'	Pg. 115--117				8:31-47	
JESUS heals a BLIND MAN at POOL of SILOAM; Pharisees cast him out of synagogue for praising JESUS for it	Pg. 117--118				8:48-59	
	Pg. 118--120				9:1-12	
	Pg. 120--121				9:13-34	
	Pg. 121--122				9:35-41	
JESUS describes the 'GOOD SHEPHERD'	Pg. 122--124				10:1-21	

Appendix A -- (Pg. 10 of 22)

HARMONY of the GOSPELS

EVENT / ACTIVITY		MATH	MARK	LUKE	JOHN	ACTS
JESUS anoints SEVENTY OTHERS; to send out to cast out devils, heal & raise	Pg.124--126			10:1-16		
	Pg.126--127			10:17-24		
PARABLE; from JERUSALEM... the 'GOOD SAMARITAN'	Pg.127--128			10:25-37		
JESUS goes to BETHANY; dines at MARTHA's house--(MARY's sis) MARTHA serves, MARY sits at feet	Pg.129			10:38-42		
JESUS teaches the 'LORD'S PRAYER' again	Pg.129--130			11:1-13 *(& Mat 6:9-15)		
PHARISEES BLASPHEME the Holy Spirit	Pg.130--132			11:14-26		
	Pg.132--133			11:27-36		
JESUS DINES WITH unnamed Pharisee	Pg.133--135			11:37-54		
JESUS continues teaching, in JERUSALEM	Pg.135--136			12:1-12		
	Pg.136--137			12:13-34		

Appendix A -- (Pg. 11 of 22)

HARMONY of the GOSPELS

EVENT / ACTIVITY		MATH	MARK	LUKE	JOHN	ACTS
PARABLE; from JERUSALEM...	Pg. 137--138			12:35-48		
FRUIT TREE saved by the husbandman	Pg. 139--140			12:49-13:9		
JESUS heals a 'daughter of Abraham' PARABLES; mustardseed & leivin	Pg. 140--141			13:10-21		
JESUS continues teaching in JERUSALEM THEN, departs to BETHANY	Pg. 141--142				10:22-42	
THEN, back to JERUSALEM	Pg. 143--144			13:22-30		
JUDAISM BLINDED, till end-time	Pg. 144--145			13:31-35		
JESUS DINES with unnamed Pharisee; heals man with DROPSY PARABLE; host prepared GREAT FEAST	Pg. 145--146			14:1-11		
JESUS defines a 'DISCIPLE of CHRIST'	Pg. 146--147			14:12-24		
	Pg. 147--148			14:25-35		
PARABLES; from Pharisees house...	Pg. 148--149			15:1-24		
'PRODIGAL SON'	Pg. 150			15:25-32		

Appendix A -- (Pg. 12 of 22)

HARMONY of the GOSPELS

EVENT / ACTIVITY		MATH	MARK	LUKE	JOHN	ACTS
'WICKED STEWARD'	Pg. 150--153			16:1-18		
'RICH MAN & the POOR MAN'	Pg. 153--155			16:19-31		
	Pg. 155--156			17:1-10		
JESUS heals TEN LEPERS in SAMARIA	Pg. 156--157			17:11-21		
JESUS continues teaching	Pg. 157--158			17:22-37		
PARABLES; from GALILEE... never weary of praying	Pg. 158--159			18:1-8		
two diff't men prayed at the Temple	Pg. 159--160			18:9-14		
JESUS returns to teach in JUDEA	Pg. 160--161	19:1-12	10:1-12			
CHILDREN were brought to JESUS	Pg. 161	19:13-15	10:13-16	18:15-17		
The RICH YOUNG RULER [in JUDEA]	Pg. 162--164	19:16-22	10:17-22	18:18-23		
JESUS continues teaching	Pg. 164--165	19:23-30	10:23-31	18:24-30		
JESUS continues teaching	Pg. 165--166	20:1-16				
JESUS returns to JERUSALEM	Pg. 166	20:17-19	10:32-34	18:31-34		

Appendix A -- (Pg. 13 of 22)

HARMONY of the GOSPELS

EVENT / ACTIVITY		MATH	MARK	LUKE	JOHN	ACTS
JESUS heals BLIND BARTIMAEUS in JERICHO	Pg. 166--167	20:20-28	10:35-45			
JESUS DINES with ZACCHAEUS/publican	Pg. 167--168	20:29-34	10:46-52	18:35-43		
PARABLE: from ZACCHAEUS' house	Pg. 168--169			19:1-10		
WICKED SERVANT [of nobleman gone to a far country]	Pg. 169--170			19:11-19		
	Pg. 170--171			19:20-28		
LAZARUS DIES	Pg. 171--173				11:1-16	
(MARY is identified to have anointed JESUS' feet at home of SIMON/Pharisee)	Pg. 173--174				11:17-31	
LAZARUS RESURRECTED	Pg. 174--175				11:32-44	
CRUCIFIXION WEEK BEGINS-(WEEK OF PASSOVER FEAST):						
3rd PASSOVER of JESUS' ministry	Pg. 175--176				11:45-54	
Supper in BETHANY: LAZARUS sits at table with JESUS & Apostles...MARY anoints JESUS' feet with oil...MARTHA serves	Pg. 177--180				11:55-12:11	

Appendix A -- (Pg. 14 of 22)

HARMONY of the GOSPELS

EVENT / ACTIVITY		MATH	MARK	LUKE	JOHN	ACTS
FIVE DAYS before the Crucifixion:						
JESUS enters JERUSALEM: hailed, 'Hosanne'	Pg. 180--182	21:1-11	11:1-11	19:29-44	12:12-19	
FOUR DAYS before the Crucifixion:						
Fig Tree is CURSED, & MERCHANTS overturned in Temple	Pg. 182--184	21:12-19	11:12-19	19:45-48		
THREE DAYS before the Crucifixion:						
FIG TREE withered	Pg. 184--185	21:20-22	11:20-26			
	Pg. 185--186	21:23-27	11:27-33	20:1-8		
PARABLES: from the Temple TWO sons; rebel/obedient	Pg. 186--187	21:28-32				
HUSBANDMAN of vinyard refused to give MASTER the fruit	Pg. 187--188	21:33-46	12:1-12	20:9-19		
KING prepares MARRIAGE FEAST but invitees refuse to come	Pg. 188--190	22:1-14				
"Render to CEASAR..."	Pg. 190--191	22:15-22	12:13-17	20:20-26		
"Who's wife, after SEVEN HUSBANDS?"	Pg. 191--192	22:23-33	12:18-27	20:27-38		
"Which is GREATEST COMMANDMENT?"	Pg. 192--193	22:34-46	12:28-37	20:39-44		

Appendix A -- (Pg. 15 of 22)

HARMONY of the GOSPELS

EVENT / ACTIVITY		MATH	MARK	LUKE	JOHN	ACTS
Poor WIDOW cast in TWO MITES	Pg. 193		12:38-44	20:45-21:4		
"You shut up kingdom/heaven from men"	Pg. 194	23:1-12				
"TITHE fruit of spirit/good... not spices"	Pg. 194--195	23:13-22				
	Pg. 195--197	23:23--24:1				
TWO DAYS before the Crucifixion: "When will END-TIME come to pass?"	Pg. 197--199	24:1-9	13:1-11	21:5-15		
	Pg. 199--201	24: 10-16	13:12-14	21:16-24		
	Pg. 201--203	24:17-24	13:15-20	21:25-36		
Everyone will see JESUS return, same time	Pg. 203--204	24:25-51	13:21-37			
PARABLES; walking from Temple TEN VIRGINS with oil lamps, and WICKED SERVANT [didn't increase coins]	Pg. 204--205	25:1-30				
Seperating the SHEEP from the GOATS	Pg. 205--207	25:31-46		21:37		
JUDAS agrees to BETRAY JESUS, & MARY anoints JESUS head in BETHANY at home of SIMON the LEPER.	Pg. 207--208	26:1-16	14:1-11	21:38--22:6		

Appendix A -- (Pg. 16 of 22)

HARMONY of the GOSPELS

EVENT / ACTIVITY		MATH	MARK	LUKE	JOHN	ACTS
ONE DAY before the Crucifixion:						
GREEKS arrive, and seek JESUS	Pg. 208--209				12:20-26	
JESUS CEASES from PUBLIC preaching	Pg. 209--210				12:27-36	
	Pg. 210--212				12:37-50	
Preparation for the LAST SUPPER	Pg. 212--213	26:17-19	14:12-16	22:7-13		
CRUCIFIXION DAY:						
JESUS & Disciples share the LAST SUPPER	Pg. 215	26:20	14:17	22:14		
JESUS explains concept of 'COMMUNION'	Pg. 215--218	26:21-29	14:18-25	22:15-22		
JESUS continues teaching the Disciples	Pg. 218			22:23-27		
JESUS reflects on his own earthly life He teaches the Disciples to be SERVANTS	Pg. 219--220				13:1-11	
	Pg. 220--221				13:12-19	
JESUS identifies his BETRAYER: JUDAS	Pg. 221				13:20-27	
JESUS issues a NEW COMMANDMENT	Pg. 222			22:28-30	13:28-35	
Peter's DENIAL, foretold	Pg. 222--224	26:31-35	14:27-31	22:31-38	13:36-38	

Appendix A -- (Pg. 17 of 22)

HARMONY of the GOSPELS

EVENT / ACTIVITY		MATH	MARK	LUKE	JOHN	ACTS
JESUS encourages the Disciples	Pg.224--225				14:1-11	
	Pg.225--226				14:12-21	
The WALK to GARDEN of Gethsemane	Pg.226--227	*26:30	*14:26	22:39	14:22-31	
	Pg.228--229			22:39	15:1-11	
	Pg.229--230				15:12-16:3	
	Pg.230--232				16:4-24	
	Pg.232				16:25-33	
	Pg.232--233				17:1-26	
JESUS enters the Garden of Gethsemane	Pg.233--234	26:36-41	14:32-38	22:40-42	18:1-2	
JUDAS enters garden, with SOLDIERS	Pg.234--235	26:42-47	14:39-43	22:43-47	18:3	
	Pg.235--237	26:48-55	14:44-49	22:47-53	18:4-11	
JESUS is led away to High Priest to be interrogated	Pg.237--239	26:56-58	14:50-54	22:54-62	18:12-18	
	Pg.239--240	26:59-63	14:55-61		18:19-24	

Appendix A -- (Pg. 18 of 22)

HARMONY of the GOSPELS

EVENT / ACTIVITY		MATH	MARK	LUKE	JOHN	ACTS
JESUS is led away to PONTIUS PILATE	Pg. 240	26:63-68	14:61-65	22:63-71		
	Pg. 241-242	26:69-27:1	14:66-15:1	22:72-23:1	18:25-28	
PILATE sends JESUS to HEROD the Tetrarch	Pg. 242-244	27:1-10	15:1	23:2	18:28-32	
	Pg. 244	27:11-14	15:2-5	23:3-7	18:33-35	
HEROD sends JESUS back to PILATE	Pg. 245			23:8-12		
	Pg. 245-246	27:15-19	15:6-11	23:13-19	18:36-39	
PILATE orders JESUS to be scourged	Pg. 246-248	27:20-23	15:12-14	23:20-23	19:1-7	
JESUS is led away to CRUCIFIXION	Pg. 248-249	27:24-31	15:15-20	23:24-25	19:8-16	
	Pg. 249-250	27:32	15:21	23:26-32	19:17	
JESUS is CRUCIFIED	Pg. 251-252	27:33-38	15:22-28	23:33-38	19:18-24	
	Pg. 252-254			23:39-43	19:25-27	
	Pg. 254-255	27:39-44	15:29-32			
JESUS DIES	Pg. 255-256	27:45-50	15:33-37	23:44	19:28-30	

Appendix A -- (Pg. 19 of 22)

HARMONY of the GOSPELS

EVENT / ACTIVITY		MATH	MARK	LUKE	JOHN	ACTS
(First 'TIME' souls will be harvested/raised)	Pg.256--257	27:51-56	15:38-41	23:45-49		
JESUS is BURIED	Pg.257--259	27:57-61	15:42-47	23:50-55	19:31-42	
Roman GUARDS posted at the tomb	Pg.260	27:62-66				
	Pg.261--262	28:1	16:1-3	23:56-24:1	20:1	
The sealed TOMB is found EMPTY	Pg.262--263	28:2-7	16:4-7	24:2-3		
	Pg.263--264	28:8	16:8		20:2-9	
FIRST APPEARANCE of RISEN JESUS ANGEL appears to MARY	Pg.264--265			24:4-8	20:10-12	
RISEN JESUS appears to MARY	Pg.265--266	28:9-10	16:9		20:13-17	
	Pg.266--267	28:11-15	16:10-11	24:9-12	20:18	
RISEN JESUS appears on the road to EMMAUS...	Pg.267--268		16:12	24:13-27		
reveals himself to 2 Disciples	Pg.268--269		16:13	24:28-35		

Appendix A -- (Pg. 20 of 22)

HARMONY of the GOSPELS

EVENT / ACTIVITY		MATH	MARK	LUKE	JOHN	ACTS
RISEN JESUS appears to the APOSTLES JESUS plants, in them, the SEED of Holy Ghost	Pg.269--272			24:36-44	20:19-25	
RISEN JESUS appears to the APOSTLES (2nd time, 'behind closed doors')	Pg.272--273		16:14		20:26-31	
RISEN JESUS appears to Apostles at the Sea of TIBERIAS	Pg.273	28:16			21:1-7	
	Pg.274				21:6-14	
	Pg.274--275				21:15-19	
	Pg.275--276	28:17			21:20-24	
	Pg.277--279	28:18-20	16:15-18	24:45-49		1:3-8
RISEN JESUS ASCENDS into Heaven	Pg.279--280		16:19	24:50-52		1:9-12
The TWELFTH APOSTLE is voted in	Pg.280--281					1:13-26
PENTECOST: Apostles FULL anointing	Pg.281--283					2:1-11
CHURCH is born: PETER preaches w/power	Pg.283--284					2:12-21
	Pg.284--285					2:22-36

Appendix A -- (Pg. 21 of 22)

HARMONY of the GOSPELS

EVENT / ACTIVITY	MATH	MARK	LUKE	JOHN	ACTS
Pg. 285--286		16:20	24:53	21:25	2:37-47

Appendix A -- (pg. 22 of 22)

www.ingramcontent.com/pod-product-compliance
Lightning Source LLC
Chambersburg PA
CBHW062058090426
42741CB00015B/3264